354-/
∂7

Outreach and Identity: Evangelical Theological Monographs
World Evangelical Fellowship Theological Commission

Series Editor: Klaus Bockmuehl

No. 5   Pornography: A Christian Critique

Pornography: A Christian Critique

John H. Court

InterVarsity Press
Downers Grove, Illinois 60515
United States of America

The Paternoster Press
Exeter, England

InterVarsity Press is the book-publishing division of Inter-Varsity Christian Fellowship.

CANADA: InterVarsity Press, 1875 Leslie Street, Unit 10, Don Mills, Ontario M3B 2M5

AUSTRALIA: Emu Book Agencies, Pty., Ltd., 63 Berry Street, Granville, 2142 N.S.W.

SOUTH AFRICA: Oxford University Press, P.O. Box 1141, Cape Town

Library of Congress Catalog Card Number: 80-7668
ISBN: 0-87784-494-1 (USA)
ISBN: 0-85364-293-1 (UK)

Made and printed in the United States of America for InterVarsity Press, Downers Grove, IL 60515, and for The Paternoster Press, Ltd., Paternoster House, 3 Mount Radford Crescent, Exeter, Devon, by the George Banta Company, Menasha, Wisconsin.

British Library Cataloguing in Publication Data
Court, John H
    Pornography.–(Outreach and identity; 5).
    1. Pornography–Moral and religious aspects
    –Christianity
    I. Title   II. Series
    261.8'33'174   BV4597.6

    ISBN 0-85364-293-1

| 17 | 16 | 15 | 14 | 13 | 12 | 11 | 10 | 9 | 8 | 7 | 6 | 5 | 4 | 3 | 2 | 1 |
| 94 | 93 | 92 | 91 | 90 | 89 | 88 | 87 | 86 | 85 | 84 | 83 | 82 | 81 | 80 | | |

Preface

The subject of this monograph—pornography—is one I would readily have avoided. It came inevitably to my attention through clinical practice with sexually disturbed patients. I was studying in the United States when the Presidential Commission Report on Obscenity and Pornography was released in 1970, and happened to attend a conference where the research was presented. It was evident immediately that the results as then reported raised more questions than answers. Over the last nine years I have managed to devote some time to researching the area further.

Pornography is an international problem. Christians who understand the topic are few and widely distributed. It was therefore a great asset to be able to participate in the International Congress on World Evangelization in Lausanne in 1974. Both at that Congress and subsequently, I established contact with Christian leaders in Europe, America and elsewhere. Travel throughout Britain and Europe, and visits to Canada and the United States have given firsthand information both on the spread of pornography and of local response to it.

It was a special privilege to be able to teach at Fuller Theological Seminary during 1977, thereby extending my research contacts in Los Angeles where so much of the pornography trade is to be found.

I find that most of the authors whose writings are cited are people with whom I have had personal contact. References to their work in this monograph indicate the debt I owe them. So extensive has the worthwhile literature about pornography become over the last few years, that I have written this brief volume in a manner which directs the reader to these more extended sources as often as possible.

In 1970, those willing to speak of the potential dangers of pornography were few. Those who risked ridicule to be prophetic were abused by the media and even doubted by many Christians. Times have changed as the predictions have come painfully true. It is now as respectable to see harm in pornography as it is to recognize danger in violence on TV. That is not enough, however. Respectability could be the surest way of cutting the nerve of Christian social concern. Just as William Wilberforce labored for nearly fifty years against slavery, we too may have a very long task ahead to abolish this new slavery by God's grace. John Stott reminds us that we are called on to penetrate society and thus help to arrest the decline in values and standards:

> We should not despise this restraining influence of Christians in the world. It is part of Christ's purpose for his people. So do not let us put salt and light, our Christian social and evangelistic responsibilities, over against each other, or disparage either. The world needs both. Jesus Christ said so, and that should be enough.[1]

J. Court
Adelaide, South Australia

1

The Challenge of Pornography

The proliferation of pornography has increased alarmingly over the last ten or fifteen years. Although it has existed for centuries, pornography has generally been taboo, limited in availability and technically poor in quality. Society unmistakably frowned upon all forms of pornography and censorship laws were enforced.

The Proliferation of Pornography

Slowly, but with increasing momentum, all this has changed. Whereas fifteen years ago pornography was hard to find, now it is difficult to avoid. The demand for freedom for adults to see, hear and read what they choose has not been matched by the corresponding responsibility to avoid offending those who find such books and films repugnant.

Most people sense that something is wrong, but are confused about the issues. Especially to those without firsthand, deliberate exposure to pornography, the complex technical and philosophical debate seems to turn black into white. Consequently, it is tempting to avoid the controversy, leaving it to those who seem to know what they are talking about. Sophisticated rationalizations repeated with confident optimism by experts in art and literature, politics and philosophy, psychology and psychiatry and even by the occasional bishop, cow into silence those who intuitively oppose pornography.

It is also true that some of the pressure to legitimize pornography comes from a reaction against earlier Christian dogmatisms about sexuality. The church's sometimes ridiculous teaching about sexuality deters many today from confronting contemporary secular dogma. Fears of appearing prudish, reactionary or sexually repressed facilitate a guilty silence which can only be overcome by a truly biblical approach. If the pressures of hedonistic and "permissive" society force Christians to rethink sexuality in terms of scriptural teaching rather than from middle-class reflexes, then we shall develop a more vigorous and authentic witness to a world desperately searching for meaning.

And it is precisely on the level of meaning, not merely on the level of personal issues, that pornography challenges the biblical and human perspective. For pornography is significant not simply because of the existence of a whole industry of exploitation, but because it represents a philosophy of man which is fundamentally not only anti-Christian but also anti-human. It raises questions about the dignity of men and women, the limits of human freedom, the purpose of sexuality, and the welfare of children, as well as the moral status of sexual deviations. Therefore, from the perspective of man as created in God's image, an essential characteristic of pornography is its evil abuse not only of sexuality, but of human nature itself. The pervasiveness of such an evil is something not to be ignored but confronted.

If the Christian has nothing to say on such basic issues, then a significant dimension of faith and witness is missing. If the churches fail to speak theologically with conviction, proclaiming a better way, then a confused, despairing generation will be deserted. This is not to say that the area of human relationships and personal sexuality is the central issue of our time. It does mean, however, that because these personal issues are an integral part of daily life, to dismiss them as secondary or trivial would be to leave unchallenged the view that man is alone in the universe, autonomous, and therefore not bound by moral principles. This denies the fundamental message of love and life proclaimed in Christ.

But what is pornography? The term is used in many ways by many people to mean many different things. We may miss the point or argue pointlessly if we start from ambiguity.

That which is sexually explicit is not necessarily pornographic. Art and literature would be impoverished by this definition. Nor is everything which creates sexual arousal in the reader or viewer necessarily pornographic. That would be to include an astonishing range of everyday things which arouse most people not at all, but for some are highly stimulating. It is not that the material content of pornography is sexual that is objectionable. Rather it is the manner in which pornography treats sexual matters that makes it unacceptable. In the words of *The Longford Report* of 1972, "Pornography is that which exploits and dehumanises sex, so that human beings are treated as things and women in particular as sex objects."[1]

The Lausanne Challenge

Along with other social concerns, participants at the International Congress on World Evangelization at Lausanne in 1974 considered pornography. In an extended paper relating to a wide range of social issues Carl F. H. Henry noted about sex that

the human need of man and woman for each other springs from an original relationship grounded in God's creative act (Gen. 2:18ff.). The family is the basic natural order of creation and a microcosm of mankind (Eph. 3:14). Parents find new life together in union: children are divinely given as a sacred trust. In Judeo-Christian ethics the origin and norm of all genuine love is God's love for man, a love proffered to undeserving sinners. Because of the wholeness of human personality, what one thinks and does sexually has consequences for the entire self in this life and the next. For Christians, sex involves considerate gratitude, personal devotion and welcome responsibility under God.[2]

He then said specifically of pornography that

Christians should publicise their views of the moral wrong of degrading sex into a cheap animal commodity. Strangely enough, socially-active churches were so preoccupied with politico-economic issues, and evangelical churches with changing persons, that neither did much to stem the tide of pornography. Women's liberation movements have protested the pornographic depiction of women as mere sex objects stripped of personality for the sake of male gratification: now the nude male centrefold has made its debut in some women's magazines. Christians should enter the arena of public persuasion, emphasising not only the adverse effects of pornography on the morals of youth, but also its offense to God.

The full answer to the problem lies both in an evangelical changing of unregenerate engrossments and in the production of a creative literature of love.

The Congress responded to this call with study of the subject and a final statement which included this paragraph:

Sex is ordained by God in the context of love, which is essentially a spiritual factor. Christians must not underestimate the damage caused by over-emphasis on sex by adultery and promiscuity to the individuals involved and to society itself. Over-emphasis on sex goes together with the loneliness of the young. There is a preoccupation with physical sexuality and this tends to heighten the loneliness felt by young people. Christians must not let go unchallenged the flood of pornography which involves the exploitation of the weaknesses of man and the corruption of his spiritual and moral nature. By attacking man in this way he is made an object of lust rather than a person made in the image of God. Pornography, in attacking the image of God in man, is an attack upon God himself. In short, pornography is a destructive dehumanizing trade which exploits the weaknesses of consumers.[3]

To approach the topic of pornography without prejudging the whole issue is not easy for one with a religious view of the world. A first response is likely to be "I know what it is, and I'm against it." By contrast, the attitude of many secular protagonists might be, "I don't quite know how to define it, but I'm for it." We must therefore seek to understand how it can be that serious-minded and rational people defend something which is abhorrent to most religious people.

It will be assumed that pornography is often defended by those who produce it for financial gain, and those who use it for their own erotic pleasure. No attempt, however, will be made to confront such obviously self-interested motives. Instead of commercial and hedonistic defenses of pornography, we will, from a Christian viewpoint, examine the serious legal and philosophical defenses. In so doing we will refine our definition of pornography, becoming aware of what it is and what it is not. This approach will also serve to emphasize that pornography is not simply dirty, and self-evidently to be rejected as evil.

The Organization of the Argument

The organization of this monograph deserves some explanation. Chapter two outlines the seven basic arguments for pornography. In chapters three through six these arguments are evaluated. More specifically, chapter three takes up the concrete argument from evidence; chapter four treats the therapeutic and social benefit arguments which assume that evidence; chapter five analyzes three arguments (moral inversion, ideological, liberation) having in common a political and philosophical tone and a demand for freedom from traditional standards; finally chapter six focuses on the important matter of civil liberties. Chapter seven summarizes the analysis and suggests practical action Christians can take in view of the increasing glut of pornographic materials.

2

The Case for Pornography

Probably the most influential defense of pornography ever published is the argument based on evidence contained in the American *Presidential Commission Report on Obscenity and Pornography* published in 1970. It is now a necessary part of any discussion of pornography and itself epitomizes many of the problems surrounding the topic.

The Argument from Evidence

The Commission was established in 1967 in response to the fear throughout the United States that harmful consequences could flow from the growth of pornography. This concern led to a whole range of studies conducted over a three-year period. Wide publicity has been given to the report of that Commission which concluded that pornography is not harmful and should be freed from the restraints of censorship. The Commission reported that the widespread proliferation of pornographic books and plays had no effect upon a person's character.

The report was based on the most extensive evidence available at that time. Research studies were commissioned to investigate possible effects of pornography on attitudes and behavior. Surveys, questionnaires and laboratory investigations sought to measure sexual arousal and behavior, as well as to identify attitudes and values of normal and deviant groups of subjects.

Studies which attempted to tap public opinion avoided the value-laden term *pornography*, using instead the phrase *sexually explicit materials*. These polls discovered only great variety and diversity. Some of those interviewed expressed the view that sexually explicit materials could be informative, others felt that they might have an adverse impact and still others believed they had no significant effect at all.

Surveys of psychiatrists, psychologists, sex educators, social workers, counsellors and similar professional workers reveal that large majorities of such groups believe that sexual materials do not have harmful effects on either adults or adolescents. On the other hand, a survey of police chiefs found that 58% believed that "obscene" books played a significant role in causing juvenile delinquency.[1]

Experimental studies involving the presentation of sexually explicit materials to various groups demonstrated sexual arousal in both male and female viewers, with younger people typically showing more arousal than older people. For most subjects, presentation of conventional heterosexual behavior proved more arousing than presentations of deviant behavior.

One experiment that has received much attention found that repeated exposure to the pornographic materials over fifteen days led to satiation and decreased arousal. Twenty-three male students displayed very reduced interest in these materials after seeing them repeatedly for 90 minutes a day.[2]

Another study asked people about their responses to erotic materials. Long-term effects of viewing erotica were not great. But short-term effects included increased sexual dreaming, fantasies, masturbation and intercourse with partners. Some married couples reported feeling more free to communicate about sexual matters.[3]

The question of the relationship between sexually explicit materials and antisocial behavior was of particular concern to the Commission, and among the major reasons for its establishment. Evidence was obtained from groups of sex offenders concerning the extent to which they might have been exposed to erotic stimuli. These findings were then compared with that from non-offenders. Personal interviews were conducted on 1,356 male sex offenders, 888 non-sex offenders and 477 men from the general population. They were distributed across fourteen offense categories, though not in equal numbers or proportionate to such offenses generally. The important outcome of the study was that the sex offenders did not report differently from the other groups, either in terms of possession of pornography or in their psychological reactions to seeing it.

Delinquent and non-delinquent youth report generally similar experiences with explicit sexual materials. Exposure to sexual materials is widespread among both groups. The age of first exposure, the kinds of materials to which they are exposed, the amount of their first exposure, the circumstances of exposure, and their reactions to erotic stimuli are essentially the same, particularly when family and neighbourhood backgrounds are held constant. There is some evidence that peer group pressure accounts for both sexual experience and exposure to erotic materials among youth.[4]

This conclusion arose from a series of studies specifically funded by the Commission, and the often-quoted study of P. H. Gebhard and others who published a large book in 1965 on their efforts to link the sexual and social histories of sex offenders, comparing the results with a control group of non-offenders. This evidence and the conclusions drawn from it are good examples of the kind of material contained in the Commission report.

Since this particular study was carefully documented and produced by authors previously associated with the Kinsey Reports, it has been cited widely to support the view that pornography is not implicated in the commission of sex offenses.

Yet another study of the social consequences of exposure to pornography was undertaken in Denmark. It was reported there that sex crimes were reduced following liberalization of the laws, and that the Danes quickly lost interest in such materials. (These findings are discussed below under the Social Benefit Argument.)

This brief summary of the majority report of the Commission indicates sufficiently that the evidence as reported there led many to believe that no harm would come from removing restrictions on the sale of pornography. Since, in a liberal tradition, freedom of speech is maintained as a right unless there is clear evidence of harm to others, a strong case was thereby made for removing all restraints on the distribution of pornography.

In Britain, the Report on Obscenity and Film Censorship (the Williams Report) appeared late in 1979.[5] This followed two years of hearing evidence from many witnesses but without funding new research. The Williams Committee had access to the earlier material together with the research of the intervening decade, some of which is summarized in chapters three and four below. It came to much the same conclusions as the U. S. Report on the grounds that the case for harm arising from pornography remains unproved.

The Therapeutic Argument

The director of research for the 1970 Commission was Dr. Cody Wilson who is fully identified with the view that pornography does no harm. Moreover, in 1976 he argued that pornography is not only not harmful but can be therapeutic. This is one of the more highly regarded arguments favoring availability: even if most people find it distasteful, it should be available for the sake of the lonely or the handicapped for whom it may provide the only available sexual outlet. Furthermore, marriage counselors argue, if it enhances marriage relationships which have become jaded, then it should be prescribed for this purpose.

Wilson argues that pornography today refers

to depictions that are sexually arousing. . . . Empirical evidence indicates that both verbal and pictorial depictions of human nudity, genitalia and sexual activity produce some degree of sexual arousal in substantial numbers of adults in our society today. Thus, descriptions and illustrations relating to sex are properly labelled "pornography."[6]

Objections to this definition will be considered below. Meantime, we should note that it represents a view of sexuality which refuses to distinguish between normal and abnormal, moral or immoral. Sexual themes are simply more or less explicit, and no value judgments are made about any being unacceptable. This perspective explains the preference throughout the Commission Report for the non-evaluative phrase *sexually explicit materials* rather than the value-laden term *pornography.*

Apart from Wilson's case for the therapeutic uses of pornography, there are many who believe that pornography can assist in the resolution of sexual problems. There may be some truth in this, but firm scientific evidence has not yet appeared to prove the point. Although G. G. Abel and his colleagues have shown that highly specific sexual cues can trigger a sexual response,[7] their careful work is nevertheless preliminary and experimental.

At a less scientific level, bold claims have been made in the British courts in defense of pornography. Dr. Richards, a general practitioner, gave testimony in the following terms:

Counsel: "This is a picture of a female in chains tied up and a naked man pointing a sword at the woman's genitals. . . ."

Dr. Richards: "This is for the public good because it produces a masturbatory situation. I would certainly prescribe this for a patient."

Counsel: "Picture of a naked man with cat of ninetails striking a woman on the genitals."

Dr. Richards: "This can stimulate a man. It has great therapeutic value."[8]

The Social Benefit Argument

Until the American Presidential Commission on Obscenity and Pornography published its report in 1970 there was little doubt in the public mind that the availability of pornography in the community was harmful. Indeed, surveys of public opinion indicated this clearly. Yet several studies presented to that Commission gave prominence to the opposite conclusion, namely, that real social benefit could come from allowing such materials to circulate freely.

It was the studies from Denmark presented by B. Kutchinsky and R. Ben-Veniste which provided strong support for such a view.

The most striking finding was that in Copenhagen, during a period (1959-69) when pornography was becoming increasingly available, the number of heterosexual crimes coming to police attention fell by 63%.[9] Ben-Veniste suggested that at least some of the decline was due possibly to "the ability of hard-core pornography to channel potentially-deviant behavior into inoffensive auto-eroticism."[10]

Kutchinsky's study provided indications that a further benefit of legalization was a reduced market for pornography. His study showed that the number of pornographic books published dropped dramatically from 1,208,000 in 1968 to a mere 116,000 in 1969.[11] He also reported on customer behavior and concluded that the Danes quickly lost interest in pornography, leaving the market largely dependent on the tourist trade.[12] To those countries becoming concerned about the growth of pornography, and at the same time keen to foster freedom of speech, such findings were most welcome, since it appeared that removal of censorship restrictions against pornography would be accompanied by real social benefit.

Kutchinsky argued, further, that if the pornography trade were legalized there would be further benefits to the community at large. Because the "international porn Mafia" quickly left the scene, reduced criminal activity could be expected.[13] Moreover, the distasteful task of detecting and seizing illicit materials would be discontinued, thereby freeing the police to carry out their other duties more effectively. The risks of bribery and corruption of police would be correspondingly lower.

The Philosophical Base
The alarming growth of pornography in our century is not explained alone by reasonable conclusions drawn from empirical evidence. Nor is it due merely to our human tendency to pervert any good thing, this tendency being fairly constant. The more familiar one becomes with the discussion of evidence, the more it appears that behind and beneath this discussion are particular assumptions and philosophical stances which are usually implicit. The growth and acceptance of pornography in our century rises in part at least from the spread and acceptance of alternative moral-

ities based on these unexpressed, non-theistic world views.

The rejection of a biblical basis for morality derives historically from the writings of Friedrich Nietzsche who, at the end of the nineteenth century, seriously pursued the proposition that God does not exist. He extended the evolutionary theory which Charles Darwin applied to biology to all spheres of human existence, including our sources of morality.[14]

The rejection of a theocentric view of the world leads to several consequences for morality. The first consequence of the rejection of a theocentric view is that people are drawn into the conceptual vacuum created by the denial of God, thereby replacing God. In an evolutionary context, this means that ethical principles are relative: if the outcome of an action appears beneficial to society, that is, likely to lead to its survival, it can be endorsed. This view has been adopted by secular humanism. In rational terms it appears to have great potential for human development, for it provides a framework for testing its predictions for human happiness. We will consider this perspective further in chapters three and four.

A second consequence of the "God is dead" philosophy of Nietzsche is that, because man is alone with no higher authority to turn to, moral standards cannot exist at all. Nothing is true and everything is permitted. The problem is that what starts as an apparent emancipation from constraint leads to despair and nihilism. This has been the experience of atheistic existentialism and has been expressed vividly in the art and literature of this century. There is a notable loss of meaning, an inversion of values, and a challenging of all traditional standards. (A good perspective on such developments has been offered by H. R. Rookmaaker.[15]) While the secular humanist is able to replace God with man and emphasizes rationality as a basis for standards, this further step removes all basis for standards and leads to a total loss of meaning. The immediate implications of this position are developed below under the Moral-inversion Arguments.

As a person sees himself not as a creature but as nothing more than a product of chance events occuring through time, a third consequence appears: final values of right and wrong disappear, for there can be no fixed categories or standards. It becomes impossible to approve anything as good or to condemn anything as evil.

Francis Schaeffer, who has explored these consequences in a number of his writings, says,

> Either man and his morality are the creation of a personal, rational powerful and holy God, or man is "nothing other" than the product of irrational forces—matter plus time plus chance.[16]

According to Schaeffer, life as conceived by modern man consists of two "stories": a lower story of reason, logic, evidence and argument, where he has found no value, and an upper story of value which once included God, heaven, soul and so forth. Having found no value in the lower story and having rejected the traditional source of values in the upper story—God—man is forced to invent any kind of an upper story of value to which he may leap by faith. Pornography is one item that can be placed in the upper story and injected with value. In an act of pure mysticism, the artist writes a pornographic story in hopes that somehow beauty and meaning will "drop" forth from it.

> The essence of modern man lies in his acceptance of a two-level situation, regardless of what words or symbols are used to express this. In the area of reason man is dead and his only hope is some form of a leap that is not open to consideration by reason.... Modern pornographic writing is explicable in these terms too. There have always been such writings, but the new ones are different—many of today's pornographic works are philosophic statements.... Evangelical Christians tend to write off such people and then get into trouble over understanding modern man, for in reality these people are the philosophers of the day.... They are writing pornographic material today in the hope that finally an ethic for the golden age will drop out. Thus pornographic writing is now put in the upper story. They conceive of pornography as the ultimate release—it is the leap to freedom.[17]

The Moral-inversion Argument

It is a fundamental assumption of religious morality that love is the basis for good relationships. This is also a central concept in humanistic ethics. It follows that willingly harming others is immoral. It is moral inversion to reverse these assumptions so that hate replaces love as the basis of relationships, and the wish to hurt gains acceptance.

Moral inversion deforms what is beautiful and praises ugliness as a virtue. It discards the spiritual in human relationships and promotes expressions of sexuality which never rise above the mechanical. It tears away the claims of modesty and privacy to replace them with an "honesty" and "frankness" which destroys intimacy. It entirely separates love from sex and demonstrates a basic hatred of all that is truly human. This reversal on a philosophical level is matched on a psychological level: experiences of love in early childhood facilitate the ability to love later in life. Conversely childhood trauma, desertion and psychological abuse make it likely that as adolescence and adulthood are reached, such experiences will so color relationships that an attitude of coldness at best, or hostility and hate at worst, results.

There has always been a pathological minority who find it easier to hate than to love, to hurt than to show tenderness. That such attitudes should be accepted and respected, however, appears to be a new phenomenon. The sociologist Emile Durkheim has identified social alienation and anomie as products of mass democracy especially in complex urban industrial concentrations. Alienation and anomie cause more people to find it more natural to hate than to love. The disturbing feature of this development is that, instead of remaining marginal, such individuals have been able to come together and through development of their own ethos become influential both in maintaining themselves and propagating their philosophies.

Access to the media and the media's lionization of the eccentric and the bizarre have enabled groups sharing an immoral philosophy to exert a powerful influence on media standards. This in turn has led to programming which suggests that moral inversion is a legitimate alternative to traditional morality.

Examples of this moral inversion in literature and entertainment are the works of writers like Marquis de Sade, Jean Genet, or Kenneth Tynan who wrote *Oh, Calcutta!* De Sade's pathological obsession was to deprave and corrupt people in such a way that they would become willing victims. This obsession is embodied today —the myth common in current pornography, that when women are raped, they end up actually enjoying the experience.

In the past, the work of writers and dramatists who have sought to expound an ethic of hate was seen as a deviant aspect of a society in which the norms of love prevailed, at least in principle. We are now in danger of accepting that immorality which arises from pathology as if it were the new norm. W. R. D. Fairbairn, a Scottish psychiatrist, while discussing individuals who have developed schizoid characteristics, describes this inversion:

> There are two further motives by which an individual with a schizoid tendency may be actuated in substituting hating for loving—curiously enough one an immoral and the other a moral motive. . . . The immoral motive is determined by the consideration that, since the joy of loving seems hopelessly barred to him, he may as well deliver himself up to the joys of hating and obtain what satisfaction he can out of that. He thus makes a pact with the Devil and says "Evil be thou my good." The moral motive is determined by the consideration that if loving is overtly destructive and bad, it is better to destroy by hate, than to destroy by love, which is by rights creative, and good. When these two motives come into play therefore, we are confronted with an amazing reversal of moral values. It becomes a case, not only of "Evil be thou my good," but also of "good be thou my evil."[18]

For similar motives, themes of sexual violence are deliberately emphasized in some contemporary rock music. Alice Cooper's macabre dismembering of dolls on stage in symbolic assaults on children, and the development of punk rock, with its emphasis on obscenity and depravity as a lifestyle, exemplify what is undoubtedly a seriously held view.

Pictorial pornography less frequently adopts such a serious philosophical position. More often it is promoted for financial reasons to pander to the sexual weaknesses of men. Nonetheless, what is portrayed reveals underlying assumptions. Material involving children, homosexual relationships and bestiality implies that these activities are entitled to acceptance and legitimacy in a society where traditional moral standards are rejected in favor of a philosophy of "whatever turns you on."

The Ideological Argument
While some favor freedom for pornography out of high hopes that the human condition will improve if only the forces of law and order are restrained in favor of the individual being free to choose, a quite different philosophical position also seeks wide dissemination of pornography.

Radical thinkers of the political left who are committed to revolution argue for free availability of pornography on ideological grounds. Taking their inspiration from writers such as Wilhelm Reich and Herbert Marcuse, they promote sexual anarchy for its disruptive impact. Pornography can serve as a vehicle to overthrow the old repressive culture. It is advanced as a means whereby the coldness of anti-sexual philosophy, said to be a characteristic of traditional morality, can be overcome. It was also hoped that the separation of bodily function from emotional fulfillment, associated with industrialized society and technological man, might be overcome by an uninhibited acceptance of unrestrained sexuality.

While it might appear that the pursuit of such goals would be in conflict with the status quo, this is not altogether so. It is also a convenient strategy for politicians faced with the need to make unpopular economic decisions to capitalize on an area of choice where people can sense increasing freedom. Areas of sexual and moral freedom have been used in this way, as Huntford has shown in relation to Sweden.[19] In short, those who see advantage in fostering desublimation include some who are content with established political systems, as well as some who seek to overthrow these systems.

By the disruption of personal sexual ethics, the undermining of the commitment to marriage, and the destruction of the most hated institution—the family—the structure of Western society, founded as it has been on Christian values, can be gradually dismantled, thereby opening the way for a radical alternative.

In the desublimating repression of the permissive society, a pseudo-sexual ideology is used to try and awaken the dead body. The cold head tries to re-evoke the warmth it had once turned against. There are specific reasons, which Marcuse has described at some length, why desublimation should be a characteristic of late capitalistic society. As the conditions of life in large cities deteriorate, and the explosive tensions of an increasingly dehumanised affluent society magnify, there is political advantage to be gained both by channelling rebellion into personal forms which can be manipulated commercially, and by increasing social provision of various forms of "sexual relaxation therapy" of the type once limited to the night club or the pornographic book shop.[20]

One of the more straightforward protagonists for this ideological position is Richard Neville, editor of *Oz* magazine, who was prosecuted in London for his attempts to corrupt the young in *Children's Oz*. His testimony before the Longford Committee is discussed in the context of its revolutionary implications by Peter Grosvenor:

One of the more dangerous features of the campaign to legalise pornography of every kind is the way it is often used to attack family life. . . . Richard Neville thought that certain of the more explicit magazines with their vivid descriptions of group sex and unusual sex techniques were liberating influences. "An orgy is an extremely healthy therapeutic activity," he declared. "Suppose you had a 15-year-old daughter, would you let her read such a magazine?" Mr. Neville replied that certainly he would. "Do you think this would encourage her to be promiscuous?" "Certainly," replied Mr. Neville, "that really is the whole point of such magazines. . . . " He saw society being restructured in time so as to get rid of the hated nuclear family (mum, dad and the kids) which was with certain rare exceptions an inward-looking and on the whole self-destructive institution.[21]

The Christian must also recognize that part of the ideological component is explicitly anti-Christian. The violation of nuns, the desecration of Mary, the representation of Jesus as a promiscuous homosexual are themes which pornographers have used in recent years in order to denigrate Christian ideals and assault the qualities most treasured in Christian thinking. One recent pornographic project, however, has encountered unprecedented opposition in Britain and Europe. The Danish pornographer Jens Thorsen proposed to create a film about the sex life of Jesus Christ and to market a script of the proposed film. Of this script Mary Whitehouse has written that

> Love is identified throughout with lust, and promiscuity is presented as the prerequisite of a problem-free society. Pornographic orgies, armed robberies, church desecration, mass sex hysteria—all these are presented as "The Way" to the happiness, joy and peace which Jesus came to proclaim. . . . Jesus, the "drunk and the lecher," calling on his followers to "follow me" and leading them into a brothel, the seduction of Jesus as whores proclaim him as "The Messiah, Son of God", all amount to the ultimate in spiritual vandalism and corruption. . . . After reading the translated script of the Thorsen Jesus film, one was overwhelmed with a sense that here we were witnessing the recrucifixion of Christ with weapons which were essentially those of the twentieth century.[22]

These themes have been most directly and obviously offensive to Roman Catholics, who, correspondingly, have been more active in their rejection of pornography than most evangelicals. There should, however, be an ecumenical, not a sectarian, response to such patently offensive and blasphemous insults.

The Liberation Argument

A related but milder defense of pornography argues for it on grounds that it will lead to the liberation of sexuality from taboos and repressions of the past. For those who reject the view that sexuality is part of God's creation and therefore subject to his divine law, it follows that unlimited sexual pleasure and unqualified sexual experimentation are desirable. Distinctions between heterosexual and homosexual become irrelevant, and bisexuality is seen as more liberated than either hetero- or homosexuality. Sexual behavior becomes characterized by an absence of norms.

While such a position is constantly promoted in the "playboy philosophy" of magazines devoted to sexual pleasure, it is also a conviction held strongly by many secular sex therapists. The current sexual orthodoxy refuses to make any value judgment about a patient's sexual preferences. What is personally satisfying is considered the criterion by which to assess therapeutic methods. This approach to therapy is entirely consistent with a value system which refuses to acknowledge absolute standards for human conduct.

The case is succinctly put by the distinguished sex therapist John Money who, in speaking to a conference on ethics in sex therapy, said,

> There are no absolute standards of right and wrong—only a series of approximations as new data, new events, new artifacts and new people require the updating of old standards. . . . There is no absolute criterion by which to evaluate a bisexual cultural tradition as either superior or inferior to a monosexual one. The very existence and cultural viability of a bisexual society does, however, require that we in our society do not set up exclusive heterosexuality as an absolute norm. An exclusively heterosexual society is neither superior nor inferior to a bisexual one.[23]

This cry for sexual liberation is but one expression of a tendency of recent years, from both within and without the church, to abandon those constraints on human behavior which arise according to traditional views from natural law and specifically biblical teaching. Hence a removal of all constraints on sexual behavior is not only highly attractive, but the denial of this freedom is understood as political oppression as well.

This is especially noticeable among those who see themselves as minority groups. The cause of homosexual liberation, for example, has been advanced by the Gay Liberation Movement in a manner which not only seeks freedom for sexual expression but also speaks against political oppression. In support of this campaign, there has been an increase of plays and films promoting the homosexual cause. There is a small but growing pornographic literature featuring homosexuality. The popular media, where homosexuals are commonly influential, seek to promote the image of homosexuality as normal and attractive—in contrast to earlier, and still evident, caricatures and stereotypes.

Similarly, the women's liberation movement has pressed for equality in a world portrayed as sexist and oppressive. Traditional Christian teaching on the role of women has received sustained criticism as opportunities for women to achieve emancipation in many areas of life have increased.

Differences in motivation within the women's movement have led to disagreements about methods, goals and, in particular, pornography. On the one hand, some women seek freedom from male domination in society in order to secure greater opportunity for personal fulfillment and service to others. They emphasize the equal dignity and worth of women as persons, and work to achieve a fuller expression of this in the structures of society. Such women typically abhor pornography as exploitative and the very epitome of the sexism they reject.

On the other hand, some women militantly seek women's rights solely to be free from male domination. Aggression and hostility characterize their campaign. Their goal is not to achieve a mutual relationship of equality with men but to reverse the relationships such that women become independent of men and even dominate them. This position logically demands a sexual literature with its own values. Because this type of liberation is associated with a call for total political freedom, pornography is endorsed in spite of its message of hostility to women. Lesbian literature, promoting women's sexual gratification apart from any relationship with men, encourages women to masturbate in order to achieve this.

Most recently, sexual liberation has campaigned for children's right to express their own sexuality. In this instance, the pressure comes not from children themselves but from adults who, for sexual, commercial or political reasons wish to encourage children to become sexually active. The advocates of children's liberation sometimes seek to free the child from the influence of parents (for political reasons), sometimes wish to encourage young people into activities that will enlarge the market for contraceptives and abortions (a commercial interest), and sometimes promote children's sexual activities in order to meet their own sexual desires (a sexual motive). All these interests can be detected in the promotion of sexually explicit literature and films which range from sex education materials (even well-intentioned sex education material has had the effect of increasing rather than combatting early, promiscuous sexual activity),[24] through the articles and advice columns of teenagers' magazines, to the excesses of child pornography where young children are used and abused for the gratification of adults.

At the extreme end of this spectrum, liberation moves away from the desire for freedom of expression with respect for the welfare of others, and insists on the expression of sado-masochism as a legitimate activity. So the writings of the Marquis de Sade receive serious attention. Central features of his writing have been expressed by C. W. Haskell, who writes,

> The three favourite preferences of Sade were sodomy, sacrilegious fancies and cruelty. He delightedly listed the fiendish torture devices of history and actually prayed to Satan to suggest new means of violence and perversion. He considered violence in all its forms a means of playing God. His hatred of mankind is clearly evident in all his work. . . . To him there is no fall, for man and the world as they exist are normal. Sade thought it highly offensive to call anything sin, and he insisted that murder, rape, theft, disease and death are all manifestations of nature and therefore beyond criticism.[25]

These views flowed not simply from his own sexual pathology but also from his logical convictions that whatever *is* is right, and since the male is by nature stronger than the female, men have the right to do what they will with women. Sadism, understood in this way, becomes an expression of liberation and is thus supported by a philosophical view based on determinism.

The Civil Liberties Argument
Finally, pornography has been defended as part of the argument for freedom of speech. The defense of civil liberties is among the most important issues in all of those countries where changes in the pornography law have been proposed. The case has been most strongly argued in the United States because the First Amendment

to the Constitution ensures freedom of speech. Some who find pornography itself distasteful nonetheless argue that an infringement of freedom of expression is a greater evil. This line of argument derives from the philosophical principles of John Stuart Mill, the nineteenth-century writer who espoused utilitarianism as a principle for social order. Because his influence is so pervasive in determining how the law should be formed in relation to pornography, as well as a whole range of related "victimless crimes," this position will be given detailed consideration in chapter six.

Summary

We have seen that pornography is not simply the preserve of the dirty old man or of commercial enterprise interested in making money out of human weakness. Certainly these have been present for a very long time, and they continue to be present. But in recent years they have been joined by more serious influences. A defense of pornography has developed as its presence in society has extended. This defense takes various forms, some of them mutually exclusive.

The main lines of argument advanced in defense of pornography favor a terminology ("explicit sexual material") which defines it essentially in terms of sexual arousal and which makes no distinction between types of sexual material relative to categories of right or wrong, perverse or normal. The general assumption about pornography is that it will either have no effect or else be positively beneficial.

3

The Evidence
Examined

A Christian response to the various defenses of pornography must not be addressed merely to the *moral* issues involved. Spiritual, ethical and biblical truths form the basis from which the *philosophical* and *scientific* arguments outlined in chapter one should be examined. We cannot be content to have ethicists and scientists talking past each other along lines which have no common coordinates. If truth is universal, then revealed truth should be compatible with scientific discovery. We should find a consistency between moral argument and the reliable data of science so that there is no conflict between the moral and scientific approaches to knowledge.

The following critique of the major arguments in defense of pornography, which takes up these arguments in the same order as in chapter two, will introduce new dimensions to the subject and thereby produce a more detailed definition. Fuller dimension and more precise definition are important because one of the problems to be confronted in discussion about pornography is what is *not* said: the pro-pornography argument conspicuously omits moral dimensions which the religious thinker would emphasize as important.

In a secular world where science reigns supreme, the main way of demonstrating the validity of a point of view is to accumulate sufficient evidence consistent with one's position to counter alternative viewpoints. In recent years, this evidential argument has been backed by efforts to manipulate public opinion through advertising and repetition of persuasive and catchy phrases. Thus either with evidence, or without it, it is possible to propagate a viewpoint which gains widespread acceptance.

Evidence Prior to 1970

The U. S. Commission on Obscenity and Pornography is an example of an effort to gather scientific evidence and to introduce it into the discussion of pornography. This Commission spent two million dollars on research designed to provide a basis for scientific debate of the issues. The report which reached the public was an interpretation of the original data and concluded that there is "no evidence that exposure to or use of explicit sexual materials play a significant role in the causation of social or individual harms such as crime, delinquency, sexual or non-sexual deviancy of severe emotional disturbances."[1]

Fortunately, these conclusions were not accepted without challenge. The Commission included Charles Keating, Father Morton Hill and Rev. Winfrey Link, who recognized that the conclusions being reached did not do justice to the evidence contained in the nine volumes of research reports received by the Commission. With the assistance of Dr. Victor Cline, a professor of psychology, a minority report was prepared which stated that much of the evidence was glossed over or ignored by the majority report.[2]

The two reports, published in the same volume (after an enormous struggle), symbolize the confrontation which is occurring between those with an atheistic view on the one hand and a broadly religious view on the other. The minority report clearly recognizes that a human being is more than merely a biological organism. Underlying the majority report is the philosophy of secular humanism.

The findings contained in the majority report continue to be widely quoted as if they were unexceptionable, in spite of a number of rebuttals of many of the conclusions. A difficulty is apparent within the report itself: while the majority report is intended to summarize in a digestible form the information contained in the nine volumes of technical research data, each research volume acknowledges that "this technical report has not been reviewed or approved by the full Commission." The protest contained in the minority report, and amplified later by Professor Cline, indicates that the whole exercise was conducted in an unscientific manner.

With the benefit of hindsight and additional evidence, it now appears that almost all the major findings of the Commission can be challenged as either inconclusive or wrong. Several critiques have been published examining the research in considerable detail, so that it is unnecessary to rehearse all the objections here. After the minority report referred to above, which had to be prepared in a very short time, Professor Cline went on to prepare a fuller commentary together with related material, in his book *Where Do You Draw the Line?* Attempts to incorporate objections to the Commission's findings in the scientific literature have met with considerable opposition,[3] in spite of the expressed wish of the Commissioners that there should be "critical examination and appraisal of these reports." Nonetheless, to those who wish to understand the arguments over evidence, other sources are now available. These include *The Longford Report* and books by J. W. Drakeford and J. Hamm,[4] H. J. Eysenck and D. K. Nias,[5] and J. H. Court.[6]

The evidence presented in the Commission's report has been challenged and criticized along seven lines. We will present here just one representative from each line.

1. The Commission's conclusions do not always follow logically from the evidence contained in the original research reports.

The report concluded that "extensive empirical investigation both by the Commission and by others provides no evidence that exposure to or use of explicitly sexual material plays a significant role in the causation of social or individual harms such as crime, delinquency, sexual or non-sexual deviancy or severe emotional disturbances."[7]

Yet the careful study presented to the Commission by Davis

and Braucht *did* find such evidence. They studied exposure to pornography of 365 people from seven different subgroups, and concluded that a positive association between deviant behavior and exposure to pornography could be shown at all ages of exposure. They stated specifically that "one finds exposure to pornography is the strongest predictor of sexual deviance among the early age of exposure subjects."[8]

2. Some of the research was so artificial as to be technically satisfactory but quite unsuited to generalization.

The laboratory study of C. B. Reifler and others involved 23 male students who were shown the same pornographic materials for 90 minutes a day. After three weeks, it was found that the students had a decreased interest in the materials. Physiological measures also showed reduced arousal levels.

Such a finding is not in the least surprising, but it is quite inappropriate to generalize from this study, as some did, that, given free access to pornography, people will rapidly satiate. The authors, in their own report, have indicated how very limited were the implications of the study:

Several qualifications must be placed on the conclusions presented in this report. Our subjects were young, white adults, whose educational level and socio-economic background is greater than the national average.... Given the opportunity to withdraw, eighteen of the seventy initial volunteers withdrew. ... The fact that these subjects were self-selected is not as worrisome in terms of potential generalisability as is their age and educational level.... Most exposures to pornography do not, however, occur under the solitary conditions of social isolation that were part of the design of the experiment. We do not know what the effects on response to pornography would be if additional variables of social interaction with individuals or groups of the same sex, or opposite sex, were added. Can our findings be generalised to younger, less well-educated or less stable populations? In order to be certain, additional studies would have to be done.[9]

Additional study carried out by H. H. Schaefer and A. Colgan[10] has confirmed the limitations of the earlier study. It is now clear that the way the experiment was set up was bound to produce habituation or extinction of the response, since no reinforcing outlet was available to the subjects. Thus the laboratory study is technically interesting, but irrelevant to the real world.

3. There were major gaps in the research. Cline notes that

Although in the Final Report the Commission states "[there] is no evidence that exposure to or use of explicit sexual materials plays a significant role in the causation of social or individual deviancy or severe emotional disturbances ... or plays a significant role in the causation of delinquent or criminal behavior among youth or adults" (pp. 58, 59), they do not mention that there was not a single, experimental study, longitudinal study, or clinical case study involving youth.... For all practical purposes significant data or research dealing directly with the impact of erotica on youth is a void in the Commission's work. It simply doesn't exist.[11]

(Though it does not alter the case, we should note for the sake of accuracy that the claim of "no evidence" is footnoted both in the original report and by Cline to mean "no reliable evidence.")

4. Many of the studies were preliminary in character and should be accepted only with caution until thorough replication is possible. Kutchinsky's studies of pornography in Denmark, in their original presentation and even in the titles of the papers, carry an appropriate caution. His three papers are entitled: "Pornography in Denmark: Pieces of a Jigsaw Puzzle Collected around New Year 1970," "Towards an Explanation of the Decrease in Registered Sex Crimes in Copenhagen: A Preliminary Report of a Survey on Victimisation and Attitudes, and Some Further Considerations," and "The Effect of Pornography: A Pilot Experiment on Perception, Behavior and Attitudes."

In the last of these studies, in which 72 students were shown pornography, the author said cautiously:

We shall not try to discuss the extent to which these findings can be generalised to abnormal persons, non-students, non-Danes, exposure in privacy, and completely different types of pornography. Whether expected or not most of these findings have in common that they cannot be considered confirmed in this study. This means, among others, that they are unsuitable as a basis for a serious debate on the political level.[12]

It is therefore a pity that so much has been made of the Danish results and so many political decisions have been made as if the findings had some established validity. Especially is this so, since these preliminary studies have never been replicated, in Denmark or anywhere else.

Considerable reliance has been placed on Kutchinsky's work in the British Williams Report, where he is described as thorough and careful. While that committee had the advantage of access to his initial reports and to personal conversations, it had to release its findings before publication of Kutchinsky's book *Law, Pornography and Crime: The Danish Experience.* That book was foreshadowed as "in press" back in 1973 and frequently since but still remains unavailable six years later.

5. Some studies got the facts wrong. In the studies from Denmark,[13] both Ben-Veniste and Kutchinsky provide evidence of the numbers of rapes reported to the Copenhagen police. Unfortunately, the two sets of figures fail to agree at any point. Nor do either Kutchinsky's or Ben-Veniste's figures agree with those obtained independently from the police department in Copenhagen. And, for good measure, within Ben-Veniste's paper, the figures for rape are given for 1966 in a table as 64 and on an associated graph as 50. (Kutchinsky gives 34 and the police confirm 50.) With such confusion, it is difficult to take seriously any discussion of trends.

Following criticism of his accuracy by V. Bachy,[14] the Williams Report (para. 6.50) acknowledges that Kutchinsky actually had "reservations . . . about the recording practice of the police" and adapted his own approach to the figures with consequent discrepancies.[15] Since his account of this is still unpublished, the validity of his alterations remains uncertain. It does mean, however, that his figures are not comparable with police data there or anywhere else.

6. There were no long-term studies. Obviously, we cannot give an example of what does not exist. It is necessary to note that within the limited terms of reference of the Commission, the time available to the Commission—two years—was too little for any long-term study to be attempted. What really matters, however, is not the transitory response to pornography, but the consequent,

long-term changes in values, attitudes and behavior.

7. The findings presented in 1970 are badly dated. The most remarkable illustration of this problem is the study by P. H. Gebhard and others, described briefly in chapter two. Their work is referred to in the U. S. Commission as being the most extensive study conducted in the period between 1961 and 1968.[16] Yet in reality, the publication of the book in 1965 occurred long after the evidence was collected, being based on interviews with sex offenders conducted in two major periods "between 1941 and 1955."[17] *All* the evidence was in by 1960.

These men, who were growing into manhood in the 1930s and 1940s, were typically interviewed some years later—long after they had committed their offenses. Hence it is scarcely surprising if they reported no link between their offenses and exposure to pornography. Indeed, it is clear that the pornography to which they had access was hardly comparable to the kind of material circulating in the 1970s. Yet the study is quoted as recent by the Commission, and libertarians continue to rely on it.[18]

In addition to being hopelessly outdated, the Commission's report has been described as methodologically faulty in several ways in the review of Eysenck and Nias. In particular, groups were not well matched, and no systematic linking of specific offenses to specialized pornography was attempted.[19]

It is no criticism of the Commission that most of its evidence was collected between 1967 and 1969, and reported in 1970. But we may reasonably question the relevance of those findings a decade later, when the whole picture has changed so much. Pornography had begun to circulate in sizeable quantities in the early 1960s in Scandinavia, Britain and the United States. It was becoming a matter of public concern by the middle sixties and hence the call for the U. S. Commission.

Since its release, however, the Commission Report itself has served as a social catalyst to facilitate a much greater distribution of pornography than ever before. Pornography was being widely distributed in Los Angeles in 1969, according to the police. They estimate that there were 18 retail outlets with sales worth $15 million. By 1975, the city had 143 outlets, and estimated sales of $85 million. Such an escalation, spread across many countries, may be presumed to have brought about social changes that have made obsolete many of the Commission's findings.

The argument from evidence is, in other words, most unconvincing. However, that the evidence was inadequate does not necessarily mean that evidence could not be brought forward to support the Commission's conclusions. We may reasonably ask, What has happened in the years since 1970? Has better evidence become available? With such a growth of the availability of pornography and so many advocating its merits, it should be possible to find an accumulation of new data filling the gaps in the case for pornography.

It is surely significant that such material has not appeared. Wherever the matter is debated, support for pornography is invariably derived from pre-1970 data. There is, on the other hand, evidence accumulating for the period since 1970 to show the harmful effects of pornography. This will be dealt with below.

What has happened in the meantime is that the back-up strategy of emotional appeal has been adopted. Repetitious recitation of the outdated and misleading "facts" has been used in books, magazines and through the electronic media by people of respected authority. Most people accept the statements of these authorities —this smoke screen—as the truth.

We must not make the mistake of thinking that those who cite such evidence are deliberately dishonest or trying to mislead people. It is rather that the supposed evidence fits their expectations and beliefs about pornography in particular and the nature of sexuality in general. Of course, those with moral objections to pornography also have expectations—expectations which are quite different. They, too, if they rely only on scientific evidence, risk the possibility of bias. On finding what looks to us like scientific evidence of the harmfulness of pornography, we must not accept it any less critically than would those who are prone to defend pornography.

The advantage of the moral position is not that it can disregard scientific evidence, but rather that it is guided not solely by the discoveries of science, but also by the immutable revelation of God. This both/and position is most important in a world which frequently looks only to science for answers and proofs which are in reality beyond the limits of science to give. The limits of the sciences, especially the social sciences, as well as their liability to error, are now widely acknowledged. Science has been wrong often in the past, but the validity of creation ethics remains unchanged.

Evidence since 1970

Since 1970, the evidence on the effects of erotica and pornography, while still not extensive, has increased and it gives a very different picture from the earlier benign interpretation of the Presidential Commission. Several series of experimental studies have been reported which, with some differences, generally converge on the view that sexual arousal through pornography can often be closely and positively linked with aggression.

At least five theories have been advanced over the last decade to explain the link experiments have discovered between exposure to erotic stimuli and the tendency to express aggression against others. The theories differ in complexity of explanation of paradoxical results. These differences arise, in part, from the diversity of experimental situations.

The first theory was advanced in the context of an experiment in which male volunteer subjects were given the opportunity to administer shocks to someone who had provoked them. (In this experiment the subject believes he is giving shocks to someone in an adjoining room, but the apparatus is not actually delivering a shock at all, the other person being a confederate.) T. P. Meyer found that those who saw an erotic film after provocation were willing to administer stronger shocks than those who viewed a neutral film.[20] Accordingly, Meyer theorized that erotic material aroused aggression, as well as sexual desire.

A series of studies by D. Zillmann and his colleagues has led to a modification of this simple arousal theory in favor of an excitation-transfer theory.[21] This model offers an explanation of increased aggression following sexual arousal by people who have been previously angered experimentally. This model has been more recently found applicable to women who when erotically aroused were willing to deliver noxious stimuli to other women.[22] It was found that erotic stimuli were more likely to generate noxious responses than the aggressive stimuli used, though this may be because the choice of aggressive stimulus material was not altogether appropriate for women.

A third study of erotic stimuli and aggression was done by R. A. Baron.[23] His evidence indicated that mildly erotic stimulation may lead to a reduced likelihood of expressing aggression, while more sexually arousing material could facilitate aggression. That is, the lesser levels of erotic stimulation might be associated with positive responses of tenderness and affection (incompatible with aggression), whereas more intensely erotic materials remove inhibitions and lead to the expression of aggression.

When R. A. Baron and P. A. Bell performed additional experiments to determine whether there might be a further increase in aggression with exposure to still more erotic materials, they did not find this.[24] They suggest that this is probably because they did not use materials of a more pornographic kind, for when such materials were used by Y. Jaffe and others, the expected incremental increase was found.[25] According to this model, then, the magnitude of sexual arousal determines the magnitude of sexual aggression, regardless of whether subjects were previously made angry. Meyer's simple arousal theory does not explain results where subjects are not first provoked.

A fourth model, a variant of that suggested by Baron, is related to work by E. and M. Donnerstein and R. Evans. Still invoking the concept of arousal, they have suggested that while mildly erotic stimuli may serve as distractors away from aggressive responses, more strongly arousing stimuli generate a higher degree of arousal, with physiological properties similar to those experienced in states of anger, and thereby facilitate aggression.[26] In line with this view, Donnerstein presented a paper to the American Psychological Association Conference in 1978, reporting increased aggression in subjects exposed to films of sex and violence.

Reviewing such studies and seeking a coherent explanation for diverse findings, Eysenck and Nias in 1978 commented,

> It appears that mild forms of erotica have tended to inhibit aggression while more explicit or "hard-core" material has acted to facilitate it. This makes sense in terms of the different mood states generated by the two types of material. Mild erotica involving aesthetically pleasing poses, or tender and affectionate

lovemaking, might be expected to give rise to pleasurable feelings which would appear to be incompatible with the expression of aggression. Explicit or "hard-core" material, on the other hand, might be expected to induce unpleasant feelings along with arousal which would be compatible with aggression.[27]
Since that review, a further model has been proposed by S. Feshbach and N. M. Malamuth, seeking to integrate the evidence of the first four studies with their own.[28] They propose a "shared taboo" theory which takes account of the impact in Western culture on sexual behavior and expression of aggression.

Their research has been conducted largely on university students, both male and female, again using the well-established paradigm of confederates who are *ostensibly* given shocks as punishment, either before or after the subject is exposed to erotic or aggressive stimulation. They have emphasized a distinction between hostile aggression (which is commonly incompatible with sexual arousal) and self-assertive aggression which brings about a reduction of inhibition and facilitates sexual expression.[29] They also make important distinctions between the responses of men and women, leading to speculation about the psychology of rape.

The essence of their model is that sex and aggression, in addition to having common physical, biological aspects, are subject to shared taboos. The presentation of either a sexual or an aggressive theme in such a manner as to suggest that the conventional (shared) taboos no longer apply, will, through generalization, lower the threshold for expression in both areas:

Learning factors may link sexual and varied aggressive manifestations by virtue of the fact that both are taboo responses, strongly restricted by societal prohibitions. Discriminative stimuli which provide information concerning the acceptability or unacceptability of a particular taboo behavior may have corresponding effects in generalising to other responses similarly labeled.[30]

Malamuth and others, analyzing the relationship between exposure to aggressive cues and subsequent sexual behavior, further show that with normal subjects, aggressive cues do not turn people on to sexual feeling. Rather they "turn off" inhibition and, as a consequence, sexual arousal is facilitated. In the same report, going beyond undergraduate students, they report on a study of male sex-shop patrons in Hollywood which confirmed their view. Given either an aggressive or a non-aggressive version of an erotic story, those men who read the more aggressive version reported feeling more sexually aroused than those who had read the less aggressive version.[31]

This fifth model makes a valuable advance in the integration of recent work. It suggests that mild and extreme erotica have different effects on the level of aggression not simply because they create different levels of arousal, but because extreme erotica breaks taboos, while mild erotica does not. A specific test of the arousal theory carried out by Jaffe[32] showed that greater aggression was associated with a delayed than with an immediate response. This result favors the taboo hypothesis rather than an arousal hypothesis. Since the displacement hypothesis of Donnerstein also hinges on differences between mild and more extreme stimuli, again the taboo theory may apply.

A move from undergraduate populations into the world of real sexual violence raises further issues. Feshbach and Malamuth warn,

> We are concerned by the possible impact of pornography in which sex and violence are fused—as in sado-masochistic encounters. For one of the most troubling results of our research suggests that men who view such materials tend to be more stimulated than others by the idea of rape and less sympathetic to the victims.[33]

Feshbach and Malamuth show that materials portraying women apparently enjoying the infliction of pain are more sexually arousing to male subjects than when such enjoyment is not suggested. This alleged enjoyment of pain is, of course, the common implication in pornographic stories of a violent kind. The impact on experimental subjects (college students) led them to this conclusion:

> We see, then, how one exposure to violence in pornography can significantly influence erotic reactions to the portrayal of rape. ... We share the belief that the depiction of violence in erotica and pornography could be harmful. ... The message that pain and humiliation can be "fun" encourages the relaxation of inhibitions against rape.[34]

In general, I find this most recent model satisfying. It brings together most of the available evidence and resolves earlier conflicts. If this concept of generalization of taboos is valid, it has serious social implications. It can no longer be argued that the open display of sexuality will be harmless and that only the glorification of violence is to be restrained. The interactions between these two taboo areas are too close. We can argue theoretically about what the effect would be if the taboos had never existed or could be totally eliminated in the future, but we should not be distracted from the need for humane social policies in the world as it is.

There are two extensions of this shared taboo theory which deserve further study. First, within this area of shared taboo there are specific taboos which could be involved but have not yet been investigated. As the taboo involving violence against women is clearly threatened, so we may predict a similar breakdown in the taboo against sexual activities with children as child pornography becomes available. The same generalization principle which seems to allow a reduction of inhibitions against anti-social sex and violence may very well lead to an increasing incidence of incest and child molesting.[35]

Second, this shared taboo theory needs more extensive analysis in relation to the responses of sexually disturbed people. Feshbach and Malamuth have advanced their theory largely on the basis of studies of undergraduates and in the context of relationships existing between sex and aggression among normal subjects. Similarly, as noted above, Eysenck and Nias express the "commonsense" view that "mild erotica . . . might be expected to give rise to pleasureable feelings which would appear to be incompatible with the expression of aggression."[36] Yet we must not assume that, because aggression and sexual expression are mutually incompatible in most people, this is always the case. It is at this point that Malamuth and his colleagues recognize a conflict with R. S. Stoller, who argues that hostility is a common element in all sexual excitement.[37] While Stoller is perhaps too general, he nevertheless writes as a psychoanalyst with sensitivity to the pathological. For the sexually disturbed individual, the distinction between instrumental assertiveness and hostile aggression may be blurred: the presentation of a wider range of aggressive stimuli would be arousing to the potential rapist, for example, while the normal male would not find such material disinhibiting. Such a distinction can be inferred from the positive responses to rape themes by rapists reported by G. G. Abel and others,[38] and by Barbaree and others.[39]

This distinction between outcomes for "normal" and "disturbed" subjects must be pressed, because it is not the normal, educated college student who is the primary threat to others when questions of anti-social acts are considered. It is the male deprived of early experiences of love, trust and opportunity, who communicates poorly and lacks social skills. While in the experiments considered above the levels of anger and aggression in relation to sexual stimuli were carefully controlled, the anger and aggression in the potential sex offender may far exceed such controlled levels. Whether we think of a high level of arousal, or a low level of inhibition against anti-social acts, or a breakdown of taboos—each or all of these conditions may already exist in the potential offender. Therefore, we cannot rely entirely on the rationality of the average man as a basis for determining what to do about pornography.

Finally, when we have considered the theories, the evidence and the implications from a scientific viewpoint, it still remains for a moral evaluation to be made. The scientist who reports without moral evaluation may see the effects of erotica as benign because no one is hurt *physically*. We must still ask, however, whether there are other objections to erotica. Common sense and scientific evidence agree that exposure to erotica increases sexual arousal and the probability of sexual activity. The moral questions, then, are with whom? and why? If one believes that intimate sexuality should be expressed privately within a relationship of commitment and love, then acceptance of casual, hedonistic sex relations, loss of intimacy and promiscuity constitute *moral* objections to erotica. While these moral objections are not scientific objections, they *are* legitimate objections.

4

The Benefits
Analyzed

Out of belief in its therapeutic value, many who find pornography personally abhorrent nevertheless argue that it should be available to those with sexual problems. If there were evidence of benefit, a case might be made, by analogy to the therapeutic use of drugs, for pornography being made available on prescription. If, however, the case is based merely on *belief* and not on evidence then there is a real danger that the argument is fallacious; indeed the possibility that "therapeutic" pornography is actually harmful must be considered, in the light of many other apparently good treatments of the past which have ultimately been rejected.

The Therapeutic Argument
Dr. Cody Wilson's case that pornography can be therapeutic assumes a definition that includes portrayals of sexuality in medical textbooks and marriage manuals, as well as works of art, such as the Venus de Milo.[1] To defend pornography, as usually understood, by the use of so broad and undiscriminating a definition only generates confusion. Wilson's use of the term *pornography* does not even distinguish healthy information from gross exploitation and misrepresentation.

Wilson claims as a conservative estimate that "one million adults [in the United States] have had the personal experience of obtaining relief from a sexual problem by means of exposure to pornography."[2] This impressive claim is based on only one scientific study—one of those carried out for the 1970 Commisssion—and the figure of one million was derived in a remarkable way. In a survey, 2,468 adults were asked about their response to sexually explicit materials (not to "pornography"). Fifteen of the women and twenty men claimed they had received help with their sex problems. Figured according to the ratio of 35 to 2,468, the number of people in the U.S. population who had received sex-therapy help through sexually explicit materials was calculated at one million. This extrapolation was said to be legitimate because the sample (2,468) was carefully selected as a representative cross section of the U.S. population. But since only a seventy per cent response rate was obtained (of which forty per cent were men and sixty per cent women), the exercise has limited value.

It might still be argued that a sufficient basis for making pornography available had been laid, if even only one or two per cent of the population is helped (or at least say they are helped). But we should also note some other findings from the same study. Two per cent of the men reported that such materials had led to a decline in personal sexual morals, and seven per cent of them said they had been led to lose respect for women. Forty-seven per cent of men and fifty-one per cent of women thought pornography might lead some people to commit rape; ten per cent of men said they actually knew of someone who had been led to commit rape by using pornography. (To those who would say we should dismiss such findings as they are only based on self-report, one must reply that this is the same basis on which claims for benefit were made in this and other studies.)

Since 1970, many more sex therapists have advocated the use of pornography to overcome sexual problems of various kinds.[3] Although there has been time enough for extensive research, it appears that Wilson is right in saying that the study he quotes from the years 1967-69 is the only major one available.

Very recently, however, some studies have reported that the

carefully structured use of erotica in therapeutic settings can help overcome problems like frigidity and impotence. Eysenck and Nias refer to a recent conference on love and attraction during which it was reported by McMullen that a number of frigid women became orgasmic following relaxation and instruction techniques.[4] These frigid women made a more significant improvement than did a control group, and the use of filmed erotic stimuli may have played a part. Women who were given an illustrated booklet showed a slightly, but insignificantly, greater improvement than did those shown a film.

At the same conference, P. Gillan reported on a study involving the use of erotica and relaxation techniques to stimulate men and women of low sex drive.[5] Both sexes experienced greater improvement than did a control group.

We should neither dismiss these findings nor consider them definitive. It is notable that in reviewing the work, Eysenck and Nias adhere to the term _erotica_ for these studies and do not claim therapeutic benefits from pornography. They argue, as I have done here, that this distinction is important and elsewhere in their review, as noted earlier, indicate how pornography is often closely linked with an increased tendency to respond with aggression.

The therapeutic argument rests on slim evidence indeed. But this is not to say that medical illustrations and marriage guidance manuals have no place. On the contrary, it is even possible that these were the source of help to the thirty-five men and women cited by Wilson.

We must distinguish between the legitimate presentation of sexual information to those who need it, and the gross distortions of sexuality found in pornography. There is a great difference between pictures and words well presented, as in marriage manuals which seek to educate, and crude obscenities aimed at promoting lust. Authentic art and literature typically protect modesty and appeal to the higher aspirations of tenderness and wonder. Pornography, on the other hand, humiliates and degrades as it denies human dignity and emphasizes the obscene. It is therefore most likely that pornography, instead of providing liberation from old inhibitions, will fail to create those sexual responses which will enrich a sexual relationship.

From the foregoing discussion it is clear that confusion arises when people use the same word to mean different things. Wilson's definition of pornography has been criticized here as being too vague and extensive to recognize important distinctions. It also studiously avoids moral evaluation.

Within the very broad classification of sexually explicit materials we may distinguish at least three types of content. There is, first, the material used for sex education and that seen in the presentations of fine art—materials whose purpose is not primarily related to sexual arousal, even though they may engender this in some viewers. Second, there is material called erotica or "soft" pornography, whose purpose is to create erotic ideas or lustful thoughts and fantasies of a common type. Such material, chiefly directed to the male in the past, is now so widespread that the secular mind sees nothing wrong with it. Nonetheless, recognizing the dangers of lustful thoughts (Mt. 5:28), we would do well to include this material under the definition of pornography offered in *The Longford Report*: that which "exploits and dehumanises sex, so that human beings are treated as things and women in particular as sex objects."[6]

A third type of material includes that which is usually classified as hard-core pornography. Such writings are characterized by an absence of the reality constraints that constrain erotica. Their aim is to create a state of increasing sexual arousal in the reader by portraying sexual relations in which all standards are violated and the primary emotion involved is lust.[7]

` The kind of materials defended by Dr. Richards (see p. 18) clearly fall into the category of hard-core pornography. It is difficult to think of any way in which such material could be therapeutic, unless one views a human being simply as a copulating animal without regard for others. Hence, Richards's statement— "I would certainly prescribe this for a patient"—gives a spurious impression of authenticity to what is a highly subjective opinion.

We may sum up our evaluation of the therapeutic argument for pornography in the words of Feshbach and Malamuth. After reviewing the responses of their subjects to aggressive pornography, and while favoring a liberal position on censorship generally, they conclude that

> We ... oppose the practice of some therapists who try to help their patients overcome sexual inhibitions by showing them films of rape or by encouraging them to indulge in rape fantasies. Psychologists, in our opinion, ought not to support, implicitly or explicitly, the use and dissemination of violent erotical materials.[8]

The Social Benefit Argument

Chapter two presented the three major arguments for legalizing pornography on a social level: (1) reduced sex crimes, (2) reduced market for pornography, and (3) reduced activity of organized crime (e.g., the Mafia).

The anticipation of a reduction in sex crimes arose from one small study carried out in Copenhagen and reported to the U.S. Commission. The evidence regarding this hoped-for decline has been critically examined by several authors and found wanting.[9] The evidence suffered from technical faults, the figures failed to correspond with official sources from which they purportedly came, and the findings have never been replicated or confirmed elsewhere.

Good comparative evidence of what is happening is not easy to obtain, but what there is leads one to suppose that, rather than the promised decline, there has actually been a rise at least in serious sex crimes generally. Arrest data in Los Angeles for sex offenses other than prostitution, for example, rose by 56% between 1958 and 1973. During this period, police found it increasingly difficult to keep up with reports received.[10]

In England and Wales, police figures show a steady increase in reported sex crimes from 30.7 per 100,000 population in 1950 to 49.6 in 1970—an increase of 62%. The same source shows that the incidence of the offense of having intercourse with a girl under age 13 rose by 44% between 1963 and 1973; over the same period, reports of rape were up by 183% and other offenses against females were up 60%.

The picture is complicated because so many changes have

occurred, both in definition of, and public attitudes to, sex crimes in recent years. Evidence from sex crimes as a whole can be used to prove almost anything. If, however, we distinguish between the more serious sex crimes like rape, and the less serious ones, the picture is a great deal clearer. Where pornography has become available, the serious offenses have gone steeply upward in frequency. Lesser offenses have generally remained unchanged or gone down. This means not that the lesser offenses are occurring less often, but that they are brought to the attention of the police less often.

In Denmark, the laws controlling pictorial pornography were repealed in 1969, leading to the appearance of a greater abundance of hard-core, sado-masochistic material. Although the Danish data in 1970 gave no indication of a change in number of reports of rape coming to the attention of Copenhagen police,[11] my own study in Copenhagen has shown that over the next few years, reports of rape reached levels higher than previously experienced.[12] V. Bachy has shown that any appearance of benefit from the legalization of pornography in Denmark is an illusion related to the unreliability of the original data.[13] The most recent figures from Copenhagen show an absolute increase in the level of reported rapes, when the figures for the years 1960-65 (56, 62, 68, 48, 61, 47) are compared with those for the years 1973-77 (87, 94, 97, 101, 110).[14] For the whole of Denmark rape reports have jumped from 173 in 1963 to 280 in 1977 and 484 in 1978.[15]

No one could have known just how great the rise in rape reports would be as other countries followed the Danish lead and allowed freedom for pornography to circulate. Such a public outcry has arisen that committees and commissions have been established to discover why rape has become such a problem. While the accumulating evidence does not support a simple cause-effect relationship between the growth of pornography and the rise in rape reports, pornography does appear as one important factor, both from evidence and for theoretical reasons.[16]

One possible outcome of this increased publicity would be to generate public awareness so that reporting rates are raised beyond earlier levels, without any necessary increase in actual incidence of rape. This argument is commonly advanced by those who wish to minimize the problem. Such a possibility exists in theory, but there are a number of objections to it:

1. Such public awareness is a phenomenon only of the years since 1975 (International Women's Year) and cannot explain the rises discussed here.

2. The evidence provided by such authorities as Radzinowicz and King in their book *The Growth of Crime* shows that the dark figure of unreported crime is increasing, not decreasing.[17]

3. As the overall level of crime rises, people show a reduced tendency to go to the police, believing no benefit will come of it.[18]

4. The development of alternative resources in the community set up to help rape victims results in women seeking help there and avoiding police contact. Official police figures therefore fail to reflect this part of the problem.

5. No evidence is advanced to support the case.

Moreover, this argument neglects the fact that, even prior to 1975 (International Women's Year), the rate of reported rape was increasing. In the period 1964-74, for example, the rape reports per 100,000 population rose in the United States from 11 to 26 per annum. During the same period, the figures for England and Wales rose from 1.1 to 2.13, Australia from 2.4 to 6.1 and New Zealand from 4.4 to 9.1. Figures since 1974 cannot be compared without many cautions of a technical kind; but rates for Australia and New Zealand have certainly continued upwards.

One study which makes it likely that increased report rates cannot be blamed on increasing willingness to report has now been completed in Australia. Evidence from a victimization survey shows that even in 1975 about one in three offenses was being reported.[19] This is a higher proportion than is commonly supposed.

There is not only a dismally similar upward trend in all places where pornography became widely available, but the increases show close proximity in time to relaxation of the pornography laws. The possibility that these trends might simply reflect general rises in the rate of violent crime has to be rejected, as I have shown that the growth curves for violent crime reports and for rape reports do not correspond at all well.[20] For example, violent crime in the U.S. rose on average 11% per annum in the period 1960-72 with the rate reducing to 6% per annum in the last three years of that period. Rape showed a 7% annual increase over the same period but, by contrast, accelerated to 23% in the years 1970-72. Pornography is the more strongly implicated in this acceleration when it is known that over the same period three countries which chose to take a firm policy against pornography (Singapore, Japan and South Africa) experienced no such increase. Indeed Japan achieved a significant reduction in its rape problem. (This is of special interest in the light of an earlier cultural acceptance of rather violent sexual depictions,[21] since it suggests that a curb on violent pornography can lead to a reduction in rape.)

These figures for the various countries are reported in the conventional manner for such data (rate per 100,000 population). A more useful comparison is achieved, however, by assessing the *percentage* increase from a common starting point and then assess from that point—say 1964. Those places I have studied which gave greater freedom to pornography over the decade showed rises in the rate of reported rape:

United States	139%
England and Wales	94%
Australia	160%
New Zealand	107%
Copenhagen	84%

Those countries which continued restraint on pornography showed a relatively small increase:

Singapore	69%
South Africa	28%

while Japan, exercising a more restrictive policy, actually registered a *decrease* of 49%.

These recent trends do not allow us to conclude a simple cause-effect relationship; nor can we reject it. They do enable us, however, to challenge the earlier promises of a reduction in sex crimes, and they also provide a basis for exploring what kind of relationship actually does exist between pornography and rape. "Disinhibitory learning," wherein the observation of specific acts lowers inhibitions against the expression of a wide range of similar behaviors, is probably the psychological mechanism linking the two.[22] Pornography may also serve as an "instigating influence" to rape. This concept suggests that someone with a predisposition to act in a certain way becomes more likely to do so when triggered by a significant stimulus or range of stimuli. It is consistent with the evidence on television violence that pornography should have similar effects.[23]

Clearly, a reduction in serious sexual offenses has not been realized through relaxation of pornography laws. Over the same period, as it happens, that psychological theory on which the hope was substantially based (the catharsis theory) has been examined more closely and is now generally disregarded. It predicted that people would act less violently after viewing violence, as deep psychological needs were met. Recent research on television and violence has shown this promise to be false.[24]

Another major promise was that there would be a reduction of interest in pornography if it were no longer illicit. Once again some preliminary evidence from Copenhagen appeared to support this expectation. But analysis of that report reveals many flaws in the data so that it cannot now be said there ever was declining interest in Copenhagen.[25] Holbrook has noted that the sales value of pornography for Denmark was $50 million in 1969, third in importance after agriculture and furniture making.[26]

Nor has the time since 1970 given any indication of a decline in demand anywhere else where liberalization has been fostered. The upward trend in Los Angeles was noted above (p. 38) and the Williams Report has documented the growth of some of the more widely available pictorial magazines in Britain.[27]

The third promise, that opportunities for police corruption would be reduced if there were no laws to be enforced against pornography, has yet to be tested. Meanwhile, police corruption by organized crime simply serves to emphasize the objectionable character of the pornography trade. Reduced action against pornography has not led to a lessening of criminal involvement. It has simply increased the profit margin and reduced the risk factor for those who pander to human weaknesses for their own gain.

It is also worth noting that to fail to stand against pornography is to allow a growth in the closely related activities of prostitution and drug peddling. In major cities, sales of pornography are made in close proximity to brothels or massage parlors as each facilitates the market for the other. The entrepreneurs also recognize that the customers for both are likely to be attracted to drugs to enhance their experiences. Copenhagen has for some years served not only as a center for pornography but also for drug trafficking. Los Angeles has a similar reputation in the United States.[28] Recently in Sweden, a similar situation has generated an unusual alliance to create a National Campaign against Pornography and Prostitution.

Organizations like the National Federation of Evangelical Youth, the Women's Federation, Home and Society, the National Federation for Sexual Education, the National Organization for the Children, and the Swedish Communist Party combined in this press statement: "The background to the campaign is the great expansion of the pornography industry and the consequent growth of prostitution. . . . Its character has become coarse and degrading and it is therefore no exaggeration to declare that this material is a serious danger to all free, equal and loving relations between people."[29]

5

The Philosophy
Evaluated

The effect of all the arguments based on alternative world views is to challenge at several levels the traditional Christian approach to sexual mores and morality. We may well find, however, that because biblical ethics views man (male and female) as a multidimensional creature—spiritual and moral, as well as physical/scientific—Christians may confidently reintroduce biblical ethical criteria into this discussion. As we will see clearly in chapter seven the biblical perspective will lead to a fuller life—not a more restricted one.[1]

The Moral-inversion Argument
The view that anything goes in sexual behavior and that all forms of such behavior are equally valid is fundamentally contrary to a theocentric world view. It refuses to acknowledge any distinction between good and evil, and is therefore amoral rather than immoral. This amoral stance is the characteristic of that scientific approach to knowledge which relies entirely on evidence and refuses to acknowledge religious dimensions to human experience. If there is no God, we have no basis for absolute standards of

morality. Distinctions between "good" and "bad" become meaningless.

But moral inversion, in its exploration of new alternatives to traditional values, goes one step further and argues that what has hitherto been proclaimed good is actually worse than the new alternative. Biblical teaching, for example, is quite clear about the importance of chastity before marriage and fidelity within it; the messages of pornography are equally clear that marriage is irrelevant and promiscuity is to be encouraged. Both Old and New Testaments teach the importance of heterosexuality as the norm to the exclusion of homosexual practices (Lev. 20; 1 Cor. 6:9). The growth of homosexual liberation movements has been paralleled by a growth in homosexual pornography—in part providing erotic stimulus material for homosexuals and in part serving to soften up public opinion for the full acceptance of homosexual relationships.

Scripture tells us that marriage is an exclusive and lifetime commitment (Mk. 10:7-9) and symbolic of the relationship of the church with Christ (1 Cor. 11:3; Eph. 5:21-33). Pornographic themes on the other hand emphasize sex in multiple arrangements of people, three or more at a time. Bisexuality is praised as more liberated than exclusive heterosexuality. Encounters are generally transitory and without sense of commitment so that the concept of relationship becomes irrelevant.

It was to be a mark of God's people in the Old Testament that they would eschew certain sexual practices common to the peoples around them. Sexual relationships with various close relatives were specifically prohibited (Lev. 18—20). These prohibitions make clear the protective function of the family, enabling children to grow up in a close emotional relationship with family members without risk of sexual seduction.

One of the tragic recent developments in the sex trade generally has been the involvement of children of all ages. In a manner reminiscent of the days of slavery, children are used as models for pornographic books and films, as well as being used extensively in prostitution. Sometimes boys and girls are sold by their own parents for this purpose. The moral inversion is exemplified by this statement by a spokesman for the gay movement in Chicago: "It's almost considered an acceptable thing for a young boy to go out and sell his body to help support the family."[2]

There is an inevitable move to even greater evil as many of these young people become enmeshed in the drug culture. Sometimes they are given drugs in order to be able to go through the perverse practices they are compelled to perform. Occasionally they are rendered unconscious and sexually abused in that state. The exploiters of these children are then left with the dilemma of disposing of children who are no longer of use to them. These children may find their way as best they can into adult life, permanently distorted by their experiences. Or, if they seem inclined to report the abuses to the authorities, they may be murdered. Such barbarism is in stark contrast to Jesus' teaching about the special care to be given to children (Lk. 18:16) and totally repugnant not simply to Christians but to the majority of the civilized world.

The Ideological Argument

If the moral-inversion position seems repugnant, the ideological argument may seem divisive and belligerent. Nevertheless, Christians must remember that they share some fundamental values and standards with many others who have not made a specifically Christian commitment. This is especially significant in light of today's political and social problems—including pornography. When Paul instructed early Christians to attend to those things that are good and deserve praise—things that are true, noble, right, pure, lovely and honorable (Phil. 4:8)—he was echoing the teachings of Greek moral philosophy. This is important because it means that Christians can cooperate with non-Christians on many issues where common values, on the level of God's law revealed in creation, lead them to similar positions on, say, pornography.

The standards of absolute honesty, purity, selflessness and love exist in the depths of human nature. Moses, the prophets, Christ, Paul and many others did not create these norms; they simply revealed them to others. As the great men of science revealed the laws of relationship between electrons and atoms, cells and organs, Moses and Jesus revealed laws of relationships between persons. . . . Because these laws exist in nature we find substantial agreement between the norms of Christian, Jewish, Buddhist and other great world religions.[3]

Because as evangelicals we are challenged to keep our minds free of those things which would corrupt, it is a real danger that we may so shun the atheistic and radical writings of those promoting an alternative world view that we become unaware of what is happening around us.

The world of politics was avoided for a long time by committed Christians. As a result, the prevailing ideologies of those responsible for government are typically secularist, opportunist and pragmatic. Christians who have had the courage to enter and remain in the political arena, confronting such ideologies, often find it a lonely and embattled experience. But the need for Christians to be politically aware is being recognized and involvement is being encouraged.[4] Without a Christian third way, we face the awful Scylla and Charibdis dangers of political movements of the extreme left or the extreme right.

It is in this context that the ideological argument engages us. There are many indications that pornography is one of the influences used by the political left to disrupt established moral standards and facilitate revolution. The pattern in Scandinavia is evident in other countries too: increasing control over social institutions and personal lives goes hand in hand with the encouragement of licentious sexual behavior. Aldous Huxley predicted in *Brave New World:* "As political and economic freedom diminishes, sexual freedom tends compensatingly to increase. And the dictator will do well to encourage that freedom."[5] The political left seeks to reproduce this pattern in non-Communist countries as a vehicle for corruption. As soon as revolution has been accomplished, however, a contrary policy with very tight constraints on immorality is applied. This was clearly seen in the years following the Russian Revolution and recorded by the sociologist Pitrim Sorokin.[6]

It has been the insight of the Swedish government to operate according to Reich's principle of repressive desublimation for many years.[7]

Throughout Sweden and Denmark the widespread permeation of pornography is now well known, though it is perhaps less well known how deliberately it has become part of the sex education programs in schools. Children from their earliest days are being encouraged to accept an amoral approach to sexuality.

The personally tragic consequences of an aggressive policy of indoctrination have been well discussed by Mary Whitehouse in her *Whatever Happened to Sex?* She draws on a great deal of factual information from Christians living in Denmark and Sweden, showing how their battle for the minds of their children is similar to that experienced in Iron-Curtain countries. The role of parents is increasingly restricted, as the state determines the style and content of education. With particular reference to programs of sex education in Sweden for children, programs which encourage an amoral attitude to relationships, Whitehouse reports that "a Government legal expert has said that 'our aim is to remove all traces of Christian morality from legislation.' "[8] Formal protests by parents in both Sweden and Denmark have been lodged with the Council of Europe Commission on Human Rights because of the extent to which their parental rights have been usurped by the state.

The difference between Western nations and Communist nations in this regard is that behind the Iron Curtain, as in China, there are tight restraints on pornography. It is in Western "Christian" countries that the battle with pornography is being fought. Unhappily, the battle is being waged largely from one side only, as so many Christians seem unaware of the implications of the policies which surround them. Through his *Man: The Greatest of Miracles*, Dr. S. Ernst of West Germany has alerted the Christians of Europe to the politicization of sexuality and to the acceleration of sexual awareness in children, no longer by the fascist forces of the thirties but by the new "fascism of the left."[9] "The U.S.S.R.," he says, "teaches that, because Denmark's internal demoralisation is so good, it will be one of the first Western countries to surrender."[10]

The ideologies would be less successful if a clear presentation of a Christian view of sex were also available to young people. The theories of Herbert Marcuse and Wilhelm Reich have led to distorted accounts of the intrinsic importance of sexual gratification apart from relationship.[11] They base their argument on the antiquated libido theory which is now more heavily criticized than the Freudian theory from which it purports to be derived.[12]

Reich maintained that the only thing wrong with neurotic patients is their lack of full and repeated sexual satisfaction. He believed that sexual abstinence for children and adolescents, and marital fidelity are pathological, creating chaos. Freud recognized that the maintenance of civilization requires a degree of self-control over sexual impulses. Developing his views in the context of an attachment to the Communist Party in the 1920s, Reich was concerned to combat those repressive forces which, through moralistic forces of shame and guilt, inhibited healthy sexual development for many. But he recognized that efforts to ease sexual burdens could also be used for destructive, that is, revolutionary, purposes.

The ideological battle will never be won by hoping the enemy will go away. Nor is it sufficient simply to object to the propagation of subversive and revolutionary ideas. If the Christian messages of love and truth were both proclaimed and lived more obviously, then the beauty of truth would be attractive to those who search for meaning in their lives. We must engage in debate and we must be active in the restraint of evil, yet pre-eminently we must live lives which demonstrate the joy of human sexuality experienced in the fulfilling and unique commitment of marriage. If our families are battlegrounds, we must not be surprised if radical alternatives seem attractive.

While taking a positive offensive against evil by living a truly Christian lifestyle, we must not impose arbitrary and nonbiblical standards on those who do not fit neatly into our twentieth-century nuclear family stereotype. One of the sad consequences of an emphasis on the nuclear family is that often the older generation and the single adult get left out. It should be unnecessary to say that, for in the teachings of both Jesus and Paul the role of the single person is clearly outlined. But frequently both the church and secular society put invidious labels on singles, thereby alienating them. We need to proclaim the positive values of the single life as well as ways in which singles can be part of a family. Evangelicals in England gave attention to this issue at the Nottingham '77 Congress of Evangelical Anglicans.[13] Without this concern we shall alienate young single people still searching for their sexual identity and spiritual purpose, thereby increasing the appeal of pornography to them.

The Liberation Argument

Like the moral-inversion and the ideological arguments, the liberation position speaks about liberation from the domination of the traditional religious and moral values which have shaped Western society. The pressure from various liberation movements, such as Women's Liberation and Gay Liberation, has as much to do with a struggle for political power as it does for sexual emancipation.

The philosophy of liberation has included a rejection of norms and an attack on traditional values in the belief that only by breaking out of customary constraints can true liberation be found. It has been the great secularist dream of the last decade that sexual emancipation would bring about that freedom of spirit which was supposed to have been denied by the taboos based on Christian teaching. This brave hope has now had long enough to prove itself and the result has been a substantial disaster. In human relationships we observe impoverishment and superficiality rather than great fulfillment. In terms of sexuality, instead of emancipation we observe an anxiety-ridden obsession.

The so-called permissive society has imposed its own subtle pressures on young people especially to conform to a hedonistic lifestyle inconsistent with their physical and emotional needs. Children needing to mature in every way over many years have been forced into sexual precocity, the full impact of which will not be felt for some years. They have been denied that sense of wonder and modesty to which they are entitled, and instead have been bombarded with all kinds of information they neither sought nor knew how to integrate.

This is not helpful in the development of freedom and full

humanity. *Progress, liberation* and *evolution* now prove to be *regress, bondage* and *counter-evolution.* Dr. Siegfried Ernst of West Germany has been a tireless campaigner for moral values in Europe over the past decade. From a medical practitioner's viewpoint he has written most sensitively of the way too early exposure to explicit sexuality and pornography undermines a child's proper sense of shame. He sees no hope of liberation through frenetic sexual obsession, favoring rather a discipline based on obedience:

> The Cross has changed the entire world. This surrender of the greatest human tensions, impulses and energies to the highest meaning in God's plan, a surrender for which the Cross stands, has since become the only real alternative of hope in the face of threats of world annihilation, mass sex neurosis and other human meaninglessness. In answer to the danger of sexual neurosis, Christ saw no reason to diminish norms of purity and self-discipline. He demanded instead the control of one's sex drive.[14]

Pornographic books and films have been used as vehicles to promote the "liberation" of sexuality. The advocacy of bestiality is consistent with the view that people should be free to gratify themselves *as they please.* Not long ago, such sexual desires were considered pathological and associated with deep emotional disturbance. Many psychiatrists would still affirm this, but it is clear that most of what have been recognized as perversions are now being promoted as mere variations. Bestiality was specifically forbidden in the Old Testament (Lev. 20:15-16). The reason for its prohibition lies in the biblical recognition of man as a distinct species created in God's image. Sexual relations with animals flouts this most basic aspect of human nature. It is one of the most bizarre tragedies of our time that our corrupt Western society will allow stage performances of bestiality and widespread pictorial representations of this, with the only objection coming from societies for the prevention of cruelty to animals!

Pedophiles (child molesters) have, with increasing boldness, sought liberation from public censure. The call for acceptance of such men comes at a time when offenses against children, including sexual abuse of all kinds, are increasing. Christ's own teachings demand that we demonstrate concern for children. His warnings against those who would hurt the little ones surely apply here. Jesus himself would approve the morality of the second principle of the UNICEF Declaration of the Rights of the Child:

> The child shall enjoy special protection, and shall be given opportunities and facilities by law and by other means, to enable him to develop physically, mentally, morally, spiritually and socially, in a healthy and normal manner and in conditions of freedom and dignity. In the enactment of laws for this purpose, the best interests of the child shall be the paramount consideration.[15]

It is a matter of public record that in recent years the United States has seen literally hundreds of thousands of young people taken into the sex industry to be exploited as child prostitutes and pornographic models.[16] At an earlier time, Christians provided the initiatives to combat comparable evils, such as slavery and the use of children in mines and factories in England. Today's challenge is no less serious: pornography and the sexual abuse of children entails, as have former social wrongs, the denial that those abused are created in the image of God.

It is not surprising that "liberationist" positions which deny the divine image in man end by advocating things which are fundamentally damaging to human beings. Taken to its logical conclusions, this position gets expressed in even more extreme ideas—those of the Marquis de Sade. The New Zealand writer, C. W. Haskell, has discussed de Sade's contributions to pornography in the following terms:

> One of the earliest of pornographers is the Marquis de Sade, who is responsible as much as anyone for the fallacy that nature, not God, is ultimate. . . . He thought it highly offensive to call anything sin, and he insisted that murder, rape, theft, disease and death are all manifestations of nature and therefore beyond criticism. In that de Sade openly vindicated murder, he is ahead of most liberals today. He was the first to advocate homosexuality as a means of birth control. To him, abortion and infanticide are legitimate, while he encouraged incest. Because de Sade rejected God, to him there is no such thing as crime.

He espoused bestiality, saying "What is man? And what difference is there between him and other plants, between him and
all other animals of the world?" None, obviously.[17]
What is man indeed? The psalmist certainly gave a different
answer (Ps. 8). De Sade concluded that "the freest of all people
are they who are most friendly to murder."[18] Consistent with this
perspective, pornography has recently taken to portraying death
in ways designed to incite to lust. Take, for example, films in
which women are sexually violated and then murdered. As hate
is pursued as the antithesis of love, so death is embraced as an
experience to be pursued as the antithesis of life. The acts of
maiming and killing as means of sexual gratification vividly il-
lustrate the total perversion of that expression of sexuality characterized by tenderness and the giving of life.

Far from being liberating, this reasoning feeds on and promotes
immaturity of at least two kinds: (1) inability to face death and
(2) inability to make and maintain healthy and meaningful personal relationships. The first point has been made by Rollo May,
the existential psychiatrist, that the intermingling of sex and death
in pornography often arises from an inability to face the reality of
death.[19] A preoccupation with sex can provide an obsessive
mechanism to reduce the intolerable tension which would otherwise be experienced. A good many films and plays in recent years
have explored these themes, not least *Oh, Calcutta!* which included a peculiarly offensive sketch in which a girl is seduced
and dies.[20] On a popular, humorous level, the films of Woody
Allen develop the theme of sex as a mechanism to cope with death.

This is not to say that such themes should never be explored.
They can be treated with sensitivity and skill. Pornographic
presentations fail in a number of respects including their function
or intent. This and other limitations, such as commercial exploitation and the offense caused, led *The Longford Report* to its definition noted above (see p. 11) and Malcolm Muggeridge, as one
of Longford's committee, to remark

For our purposes, the general characteristics of pornography
may be taken as being the use of eroticism for ulterior purposes.
It embraces, on the one hand, violence and sexual perversion

and, on the other, smuttiness and obscenity. Most often commercial motives are present.[21]

If, indeed, the sexual preoccupation is in part a defense against confronting the reality of death, then the Christian has an added reason for confronting pornography. Our message of hope for those with no hope is a straight alternative which must be proclaimed in opposition to this escapist philosophy.

Second, pornographic themes do not represent liberation in personal relationships. Instead, they exemplify a total reversal of all that is known about sexual development into maturity. An individual, progressing from childhood to adulthood, passes through various stages of psychosexual development. It is possible to be fixated at any stage, thereby failing to progress further into mature development. Freud considered the child to be "polymorphously perverse," that is, able to gain sexual pleasure (using "sexual" in a very broad sense) from many different situations. By contrast, maturity, according to Freud, was characterized by learning *specific* cues for sexual satisfaction and by developing a capacity for special and close relationships. The practices which are so praised—such as masturbation, homosexual acts and various perversions—are those which are found in people with immature and warped sexuality. There is a significant irony in the use of the phrase "adult bookshop" or films "for adults only" when what is being marketed is carefully designed to gratify immature and perverted customers unable to enjoy adult human relationships.

Pornography, insofar as it denies the need for human relationships and emphasizes isolated sensual feelings, appeals to those whose sexual maturing process has been thwarted or distorted. Moreover, for those who have failed to mature and cannot see what sexuality could be, the idea of sex-in-relationship produces anger and frustration. This colors their sexual fantasies such that a wish to hurt and be hurt becomes a common theme. This is particularly obvious in the literature of sado-masochism, but the themes of hate and hostility are prevalent generally in pornography. Humiliation, degradation and doing physical harm are presented as the means of achieving sexual gratification. Several of David Holbrook's books provide profound insight into this subject, notably *The Pseudo-Revolution, Sex and Dehumanisation* and the *Masks of Hate*.[22] The following is Holbrook's own summary of his thesis:

> The champions of pornography make out that what they are trying to remedy are the inhibitions of our instincts through prudish traditions—they are trying to "release" us. They are trying, they claim, to enable us to be more vital and feeling—to be "ourselves" more, in the sexual realm. And yet, as Khan says, what pornography achieves is the opposite. In it, the images and words "usurp" the natural functions of the instinct. Instead of natural, loving feelings, moving towards "meeting" another human being, we have an intense mental concoction of often brutal imagery—as in the cinema where rape, and other gross acts of sadism are now frequent. The effect of these mental brutalities is to "disregard the person and being of the characters." We may observe this, even in "girlie" magazines, in which the titillating way the girl is discussed, and her photographic exploitation as an object, destroy her personal unique qualities. This is the objection to the use of nudity in advertisements, too. It makes woman into a commodity thing. In all pornography she is humiliated and subjected to contempt as a mere sex object. In her image, humanity itself is degraded, by being deprived of value and subjected to hate, as the Jew or Negro is degraded in racist propaganda. Guilt and fear are not dispelled by pornography: on the contrary, it encourages us to enjoy hate in our attitudes to sex and to have contempt for other people, especially women.[23]

Although pornography is an offense against humanity in general (Holbrook uses the word *man* in its generic sense—including women and men), Holbrook makes clear that the deepest offense is against women in particular. Within the women's liberation movement there is now a major division of opinion on how to respond to pornography. Some still defend pornography on grounds of freedom of speech. But increasingly they are seeing that the messages of pornography are hostile to the dignity of women. The pornography industry rests largely on the exploitation and humiliation of women by men and for masculine lustful entertainment: it presents women as sex objects to be used, abused and discarded. The realization of this has now resulted in many women rising up against this collective sexual insult.

A British psychiatrist relating pornography to the status of women, commented that the central theme of pornography involves the degradation of women.[24] He sees this arising from men's fear, dread and envy of women, who are seeking to enhance their status vis-a-vis men. As men feel threatened by a challenge to their own status, so they may develop fantasies by which to demean and degrade women.

Many others have also emphasized this element of degradation which so completely denies the loving relationship which sexuality was intended to fulfill. Professor R. Stoller, a Los Angeles psychiatrist, believes that there is always a victim in pornography: the production of pornographic pictures involves the exploitation of the needs of those who are photographed as well as those who buy the finished product, making each oppressed, not liberated.[25]

Women who have recognized the degradation of their sex in pornography are becoming increasingly vocal in opposition. Feminists like Diana Russell[26] and Susan Brownmiller[27] respond angrily, and rightly so, to the dehumanization and humiliation of women in pornography.

From a women's publication in Berkeley, California comes this observation in relation to punk rock:

What is punk rock's implication as far as women are concerned? Punk rock perpetrates the myth that women are victims, that women like to be victimized, that women expect to be victimized, and that women are easy targets for violent behavior. For example, punk rock group Kiss' recent album "Love Gun" features the group (all male) dressed in black leather outfits standing above a group of similarly clothed women who are crouched below, fawning up to them. Most important of all, by glamorizing violence, punk rock trivializes the critical problem of assault, battery and/or rape of women by men. Punk rock should not be taken lightly or shrugged off as a temporary, passing fad. Recognizing that rock music influences societal thinking and mores, we believe punk rock contributes to a climate in which violence is viewed as fun, entertaining and normal.[28]

Women seeking to defend the dignity of women know that "liberation" in pornographic and punk rock terms is not liberation at all. "Freedom to assault and do violence to others is not freedom. The relative absence of a similar appropriate response from *Christian* women may in part indicate less awareness of the savage assault being perpetrated. It may also signify a fear of identifying with others whose views in many respects differ greatly. Yet none of us can in good conscience simply "pass by on the other side." As we consider the way women are currently abused in pornographic books, films and music as well as in reality, the parable of the Good Samaritan reminds us of Jesus' call to care for those who have been savagely attacked. Our neighbors in the world desperately need our solidarity with them against the "thieves" of pornography. They need also to hear the good news of Jesus Christ as the liberating gospel of love.

Summary

Except for the civil liberties argument, the arguments for pornography posed in chapter two have been examined critically in outline. Some scientific and Christian responses have been offered both as rebuttals and as suggestions for positive moral initiatives. Where the material deserves much fuller treatment, and major sources are available, reference has been made to reliable texts which the reader should consult.

As an outcome of re-examining these arguments, I maintain that we must reject a bland definition of pornography. Central components of pornography are (1) the denial of the humanness of persons, treating people as objects, and (2) the stimulus to lust in the absence of a loving relationship. In addition, there is in pornography a rejection of moral standards in relation to sexually deviate practices and a deliberate distortion of reality in order to present false messages about sexuality. What is explicitly advocated in hard-core pornography, and more subtly in soft pornography, is that hate and hostility, rather than tenderness and loving commitment, are the avenues to freedom and fulfillment.

The Catholic Archbishop of Toronto issued an open letter of concern in 1976, expressing much of the problem of pornography and calling Christians to action:

> It is through our God-given sexuality that we as human beings can reach out to one another in love. It is in sexual union that a couple can express to one another tenderness, intimacy and permanent fidelity. The public and profitable exploitation of the sexual, so common around us, is a direct betrayal of the basic value of sexuality itself. What is sometimes referred to as the "playboy philosophy" of sexuality, using and discarding another person with "no strings attached," is not a form of freedom but enslavement. What was intended to be most precious becomes almost trivial. What was created to be most deeply personal is dehumanised.[29]

Pornography represents a view of sexuality which is the very antithesis of a Christian and humane view. It totally omits that interpersonal dimension of a loving relationship for which our sexuality was intended. Equally, it omits that spiritual dimension without which sexuality becomes shallow. Bishop Daly of New Zealand writes,

> Sex in man is never merely biological or physiological. It is marked by man's hunger for eternity, for immortal existence, for union with God. Sex in man reveals to him an emptiness and need for love which only God can finally fill, a capacity for love of which only God can be the source.[30]

It is because the moral view of man, based on an awareness of his spiritual nature, is richer and more truly human than secular alternatives that we can more readily identify the impoverishment and assault on human dignity that pornography represents. We must therefore object to pornography not because we think sex is dirty and unmentionable, but because it is sacred and should not be degraded. We stand not *against* freedom, but *for* that freedom which comes from maturity, balance and a sexuality with spiritual foundations.

6

The Civil Liberties Case Evaluated

The civil liberties argument for the dissemination of pornography is one of the more difficult arguments to counter from a Christian standpoint. The reason for this is that Christians are in sympathy with the conviction that each individual is entitled to certain basic civil rights. We may prefer to emphasize the responsibilities accompanying those rights, but the rights are important.

Christians have, over the centuries, been in the forefront to combat evils such as slavery and industrial exploitation, though the work of men like William Wilberforce and Lord Shaftesbury generally received less support from Christians than it deserved. In the twentieth century, evangelicals have been less prominent in fighting for social justice, but at recent conferences a renewed awareness of the need for social and political involvement is apparent.[1]

Christian involvement in the social and moral issues of the day is often set within a pluralistic society where many competing philosophies vie for attention. In the West, Christian beliefs together with democratic principles of freedom of expression have permitted a diversity of views on how society should be ordered.

Secular Humanism

Among this diversity, the most vocal of alternatives to a view of society deriving from Christian assumptions is that promoted by secular humanism. This form of humanism is not to be confused with that religious humanism developed by men such as Erasmus, Melanchthon and Luther. The secular humanism of the twentieth century first made an impact through the Humanist Manifesto of 1933 and then again with the Humanist Manifesto II of 1973.[2] It specifically rejects the existence of God and affirms that there is no theological basis for ethics. For many today, rational man usurps the place of God and an influential creedal statement in the form of the Humanist Manifesto replaces the Christian creed. Humanist organizations, while not numerically large, express their views extensively through the mass media, and through organizations such as the American Civil Liberties Union and its counterparts in other countries.

Although secular humanists have high aspirations and fine ideals, many of their prescriptions for society run contrary to those which a Christian would advocate because their basic assumptions about human nature are contrary to a biblical view of man. Because they reject the concept of sin, secular humanists are optimistic about a person's capacity to change for the better, without assistance. They also reject any belief in God as merely superstitious. Thus, according to them, man is autonomous and without the perspective of a life after death. Man must make the best of it in a world that is continually changing socially and morally.[3]

Against this background has developed an emphasis on civil liberties which is sometimes congruent with Christian values but often utterly contrary. If human beings are on their own, if there is no God, if there are no abiding moral principles, and if we are best served by following reason alone, then there is no basis for any person or group to tell another person or group what they ought to do. Emphasizing the rights of each person to determine his or her own behavior, provided it is of no consequence to others, the secular humanist asks, "What right have you to force your views on anyone else?" From a secular viewpoint, the question is reasonable enough; neither does the religious person wish to intrude on the private behavior of others. Much of the difference arises from disagreement about how far our behavior is in fact of no consequence to others.

We can easily be confused by the apparent reasonableness of this position unless we recognize that the very assumptions underlying secular humanism preclude belief in the existence of God, in a moral universe where right and wrong can be determined, and in a set of revealed principles to guide mankind. In radical contrast to the Christian belief in man's sinful nature from which we cannot save ourselves, Manifesto II states, "No deity can save us; we must save ourselves."

This confrontation of two radically opposed, alternative sets of assumptions comes to focus in the area of so-called victimless crimes, of which the trade in pornography is one.[4] Until recently the strongest support for decriminalization of pornography has come from the humanist lobby. As the exploitative character of pornography has become apparent, however, opposition to it has grown within humanist groups. Some of those who vigorously champion freedom of expression have opposed the extremes of contemporary pornography because of their commitment to "the preciousness and dignity of the individual person" and to the pursuit of "life's enrichment despite debasing forces of vulgarization, commercialization, bureaucratization and dehumanization."[5]

Civil Liberties
The debate has been most vigorous in the United States, where the First Amendment to the Constitution explicitly guarantees freedom of expression, but the issue is the same in other countries. The case for freedom to publish without restraint rests heavily on the case for civil liberties, and the Christian must be sensitive to the importance of the latter. At a time when many feel that their personal freedom is often restricted by government and oppressed by bureaucracy, it is peculiarly attractive to have at least one area of life free from external and often apparently arbitrary restraints. The freedom for adults to see, hear and read what they please has been a popular cry for the last decade or so. If it can operate with-

out associated harm, the principle should be defended.

Paradoxically, the case *against* unrestricted freedom to publish is also entirely consistent with a call for civil liberties. Many who once intensely disliked any idea of restriction of freedom to publish have become disenchanted with the very uncivil liberties being taken in the name of freedom. Men and women of the arts, once ardently anti-censorship, now speak regretfully of the decline in quality, especially in literature and films, and wonder whether the pendulum has swung too far. At least part of the argument against pornography is on grounds of cultural impoverishment.

The late Sir Alan Herbert, writer, politician and champion of artistic freedom, ultimately came to regret his success in liberalizing the obscenity law in England. He wrote to the London *Times* to say how saddened he was that "the worthy struggle for reasonable liberty for honest writers should have ended in establishing a right to represent copulation, veraciously, on the public stage."[6] He was apparently suggesting that, however difficult or unattractive the task, *some* lines must be drawn.

Irving Kristol, author and academic, has several times pursued a similar point in the light of recent abuses of the First Amendment. Writing from a liberal persuasion, and as one sensitive to the need for freedom to communicate, he asks, "Can a liberal be for censorship?" Unless one assumes that being a liberal *must* mean being indifferent to the quality of life, then the answer has to be: "Yes, a liberal can be for censorship—but he ought to favor a liberal form of censorship."[7]

Fears of return to the old repression can be colorfully portrayed by those with a reputation at stake or a fortune to lose, but these should not deter the serious thinker from asking where we have come to, and how, and where we are going. As a society, are we wise to pursue a laissez-faire approach to freedom of expression, as many humanistic psychologists advocate, or do we recognize that all freedoms depend on a judicious balancing of benefits against harm?

The importance of freedom for adults to see, hear and read what they choose must not be overestimated or made an absolute freedom. Even the most ardent advocates of such freedom acknowledge the need for some constraints.[8] Prohibitions against libel and incitement to crime and racial conflict are widely regarded as necessary, and the long-standing law against blasphemy, recently tested in the British courts, looks like an ongoing issue.[9]

The illogicality of the defense of pornographic material can be exposed in many ways, not least through a comparison with areas which are still restrained—such as racially or ethnically defamatory material. In the British Columbian Parliament, for example, the Socialist member for Vancouver-Burrard, Rosemary Brown, vented the anger of many women against pornographic intrusions into the civil liberties of women, quoting the action of feminists in Los Angeles:

> They took, for example, the Jews. They said that when someone opened a store in Los Angeles that carried literature that was pro-Nazi and anti-semitic, the whole world exploded. A group of people got together and attacked the store.... When a store opens with material that is anti-woman, what happens? You put on your dark glasses, you pull your hat over your eyes and you rush in and you buy up the stuff.[10]

In such a perspective as this, Christians and secular humanists may find common ground. Though their proposed solutions may differ quite markedly, both may find in Brown's argument good reasons for objecting to pornography in practice and even in theory.

In addition to secular humanist arguments, the utilitarian philosophy of John Stuart Mill,[11] published over a century ago, forms the basis for the civil liberties position. Those of a liberal political persuasion typically emphasize Mill's insistence that no laws impinge on personally satisfying behavior which has no adverse consequences for others. That emphasis was greatly needed when he wrote and provides principles no less important today.

There has nonetheless been a tendency in recent debate over freedom of speech to take less than adequate account of the constraints on freedom which he also advocated. First, the rights of adults exist within the context of the need to protect the young and the vulnerable. Second, the freedom of some adults to choose an option should be matched by the freedom of others *not* to have that option offensively displayed or thrust upon them. And both of these are subject to the general principle that this freedom exists provided there is no harm to others. These three provisos deserve re-examination now that there has been a major expansion of the freedom of publishers and producers. Has this been matched by a corresponding freedom to be enjoyed at the receiving end?

Protection of the Young

Here is Mill's first proviso on freedom:

The only purpose for which power can be rightfully exercised over any member of a civilised community, against his will, is to prevent harm to others. . . . This doctrine is meant to apply only to human beings in the maturity of their faculties. . . . Those who are still in a state to require being taken care of by others, must be protected against their own actions as well as against external injury.[12]

Mill himself did not deduce from this principle that censorship should be exercized. Nor did he live in a society where intrusive and widespread pornography was influencing the development of young people.

But while many countries have seen the need for laws protecting the young, efforts to incorporate this principle of protection into legislation while preserving adult freedom have been notably unsuccessful. Age restrictions for films are notoriously poorly observed. Attempts at family-hour television fail because so many young children remain viewing till late at night. Age restrictions on the sale of books do nothing to halt the distribution among young people after the sale has been completed—indeed, such restricted material then has the added attraction of being illicit.

In the Abelson National Survey of Youth and Adults presented to the American *Presidential Commission Report on Obscenity and Pornography* (1970), over half of the consumers reported receiving erotic materials secondhand from others rather than purchasing them personally. Among females, girls aged 15 to 20 viewed erotic materials most.[13] Since that report, it has become clear that the total exposure of juveniles to pornography has greatly increased. In addition, the increased exploitation of children in pornographic books and films over the last few years dramatizes the degree to which children's welfare is now callously and insidiously disregarded. The extent to which children are being abused in magazines stressing incest and pedophilia is revolting equally to those with strong libertarian convictions and to those of more conservative persuasion. An estimated 30,000 young people are being used in the pornography industry in Los Angeles alone.[14]

To restrain such abuses would impinge on adult freedom. But many people, especially psychiatrists, believe that the risks inherent in the present practice far outweigh the potential problems of censorship. Many adult consumers of child pornography are seriously psychologically disturbed; the children used in the industry, already vulnerable, are high-probability risks for later adult disturbance. The belief that the availability of fantasy material might somehow reduce the problems has proved to be an attractive but unfounded hypothesis.[15]

Freedom to Choose

Mill's second proviso affirms that "the only freedom which deserves the name is that of pursuing our own good in our own way, so long as we do not attempt to deprive others of theirs, or impede their efforts to obtain it."[16]

"You don't have to read it." "You don't have to go if you don't want to." "You can switch off if you are offended." These and other clichés, based knowingly or unknowingly upon Mill's principle, have been used to justify a situation where the tastes of a small minority have progressively infused the whole culture. On the assumption that no one's freedom is thereby impaired, violence and obscenity fill the media, despite the fact that this material does not reflect the choice of the average adult. Whenever indicators of public opinion have been taken in recent years, there has been overwhelming support for a greater degree of restraint. Many adults find that the sale of pornography on bookstall displays is offensive and limits their freedom of choice, in that much better material is, as a consequence, absent. At a secondary level, and apart from direct personal contact with it, violence, profanity and obscenity in the media have a "ripple effect" on the whole culture such that norms, mores and expectations shift subtly.

Many of the changes in media standards have occurred not because of democratic choice, but in spite of it. The obscenity laws in Britain, changed in 1959 with a view to more effective control, have suffered from legal legerdemain, as well as from the now notorious protection racket uncovered among London police.[17] Legislation governing films in Britain has also been unable to deal with increasingly exploitative productions. Current enforcement practice involves a confusing combination of central machinery with advisory but no legal status, and the statutory powers of local councils which are rarely exercised.[18] In all these ways freedom of choice has been frustrated.

Ambiguity of standards, legislation and its execution necessarily militate against geniune freedom of choice by the majority. The whip is in the hands of those with vested interests, unscrupulous enough to manipulate confusion to personal advantage. In the United States it is clear that much of this advantage lies within the criminal subculture. Books, magazines and films are subject to protection rackets, Mafia control and an associated subculture of violent crime which undermines even the very ordinary expectations of daily life. True freedom to choose will develop when outmoded and confusing laws give way to clarity of definition which guide publisher and consumer alike.

Provided There Is No Harm

Much of the liberalization of media has been achieved with conscious awareness that there remains the responsibility to avoid harm. Generally, following Mill, this has been related to physical harm with a studious refusal to acknowledge the whole area of psychological harm,[19] and specifically rejecting the relevance of moral harm. The possibility of psychological harm arising through modeling, through subliminal techniques, as well as through the impact of advanced media technology, was not something Mill could have foreseen.

Contemporary liberals, however, have no excuse for being anachronistic or simplistic. The case for violence in the media rested on the catharsis hypothesis: it was thought that viewers would have a reduced tendency to *act* violently after *viewing* violence. In the area of sexuality, mechanisms like sublimation or displacement were invoked to explain why the sexual pervert would become less of a social problem if he happily and innocuously isolated himself in the fantasy world of pornography. Not only was there no evidence of harm, but the new liberation was to be positively beneficial: fewer sex crimes, happier perverts using material therapeutically and the whole population emancipated by its honest and open acceptance of sex and violence both in the media and as fit subjects for cocktail conversation—all were optimistically predicted.

Few today still believe that the surfeit of violence on TV has been for the public good. The catharsis theory has been disposed of, and the imitation of violence by a significant proportion of viewers is beyond reasonable doubt.[20] The belief that serious sex crimes might go down has similarly proved false. In the Western world the question now is how to stop the rapid escalation of such offenses. Far from retiring quietly, the perverts have come out of hiding and have been joined by many who might otherwise never have become offenders. The original hope was based on false data, whereas the present reality is painfully evident. While there are many factors accounting for these changes in crime and morals, it is no longer wise to dismiss widely available pornography as one of them.

The Williams Report in Britain has succeeded in rejecting the view that pornography can be harmful, but only by ignoring substantial parts of the evidence and distorting others, just as the Presidential Commission did in America in 1970 when Cline found it necessary to conclude:

A careful review and study of the Commission majority report, their conclusions, and the empirical research studies on which they were based reveal a great number of serious flaws, omission and grave shortcomings which make parts of the report suspect and to some extent lacking in credibility. Readers of the report are at the "mercy" of the writers of that report, and must assume that the evidence is being presented fairly and in good faith on both sides of this issue. . . . Yet, findings from seriously flawed research studies or findings which do not follow from the data are sometimes presented as fact without mentioning their very serious limitations.[21]

These accusations apply also to the Williams Report.

The therapeutic argument is still popular not because of the evidence but in spite of it. In the only serious study of this idea, no more than 2% of the people surveyed reported benefit from seeing sexually explicit materials. But in the remaining 98%, much harm may have been done.[22] If a contraceptive pill, or indeed any medical therapy, had the same degree of reliability, it would not even survive therapeutic trials.

No doubt there are many more dimensions to the question of civil liberties and pornography, but few of them go beyond opinion into measurable data. The status of the civil liberties of the average citizen has not been enhanced by the policies which promised so much. The ideologue dismisses evidence as irrelevant; but rational consideration of the evidence leads to the belief that we have gone past the point of healthy balance. Freedom for a few has become oppression for many.

Already in 1972 Professor Eysenck (no enemy of civil liberties) could see that

it cannot any longer be argued with any degree of conviction that pornography, or the portrayal of violence, has no effect on the behavior of the people who see these things on the screen, or read about them in books and magazines. . . . Both behavior and emotional reactions are affected and the effects are not transitory. The evidence is admittedly indirect, but that is not really a valid point of criticism: much scientific evidence in the "hard" sciences is of this kind, and is readily accepted on the same level as direct evidence. . . . What the argument is about is simply the nature of the society in which we wish to live, and in which we wish our children to live—neither more nor less.[23]

Christians in contemporary society should respect the principles advanced in favor of civil liberties in society, and yet recognize that civil liberties cannot create a truly free society. They provide a secular basis for law and order in society and they usefully distinguish between sin and crime: there are, after all, real limits beyond which the law must not be invoked, spheres into which it must not intrude. By personal choice, lifestyle and communication, Christians are committed to a standard of ethics higher than could ever be demanded by legislation.[24]

At a philosophical level, it has been questioned whether the arguments relating to "victimless" crimes can ever really work out in practice. A. Wertheimer, analyzing the concept in the light of Mill's doctrine, concludes: "It is not only that Mill's principle does not work, but that he was wrong to think he could develop such a principle."[25] The true humanist, the Christian and anyone else who is concerned about life in its full dimension will inevitably have reservations about the way in which harm is interpreted too narrowly—confined to physical harm when psychological and spiritual aspects also deserve attention.

Secular humanism rejects the idea of one person taking a protective or paternalistic interest in the affairs of others. As Humanist Manifesto II puts it, "Short of harming others or compelling them to do likewise, individuals should be permitted to express their sexual proclivities and pursue their life-styles as they desire."[26] In the biblical view, by contrast, we are to be our brother's keeper (Gen. 4:8-9; Lk. 10:37). We are not only to avoid doing harm, but we must actively and positively seek the welfare of our neighbor. That is, we are certainly called to brotherhood at a personal level, and we must continue to explore whether and how such a principle can find expression in laws.

Certainly we must recognize limits in the extent to which legislation can and should be involved in the control of pornography. Legislation can do little to influence the underlying problems of human weakness which create the demand. Nor can it be relied upon as the tool to enforce morality. Nonetheless, it can and sometimes should be used to re*inforce* existing standards of morality.[27] Perhaps Martin Luther King, Jr. was right in saying that "the law cannot change the heart but it can restrain the heartless."[28]

When the law is not used to avoid the harm seen by the Christian, we are still obligated individually and collectively to work toward justice and the adoption of biblical standards of morality. The task of government is to give effect to the general will of God (Rom. 13:1-7). Even if we have no possibility of altering the laws, we must still testify to God's will by the way we live (1 Pet., passim).

7

What Then Shall
We Say and Do?

After reminding the Roman Christians that they were no longer
under law but under grace, Paul challenged them to consider how
they would deal with sin. "Are we to continue in sin that grace
may abound? By no means!" (Rom. 6:1). Or as J. B. Phillips so colorfully puts it, "What a ghastly thought!" This injunction to put away
sin and walk in newness of life applies at a collective level, as well
as the individual.

As we look at the evils of our day, including the widespread
dissemination of pornography, what shall we say? Shall we say it is
not our business, and people should be free to go to hell in their
own way? Shall we say the whole thing is a trivial issue and allow
it to surround us, pervade our thoughts and corrupt our minds?
Shall we continue with pornography, so that the Mafia may flourish? So that some may be satiated with sexual perversion?

The Nihilism of Pornography
If Christians are to put away sin and prove to be neighbors to others,
then as we care for their souls, we must not disregard their minds
and bodies. Rather, we must marshal our arguments for serious

rational and spiritual confrontation with evil, so that we may both counter the prevailing destructive impact of pornography and replace the attitudes which foster it with those loving, caring responses which alone can eliminate the hunger for such material.

1. The first thing we can say, then, is that pornography is *anti-life*.[1] To reject pornography is not to be negative toward life. On the contrary, it is pornography itself which is nihilistic, reductionist and destructive. It is a negative influence in society and in personal lives. Actively countering such a force, therefore, is positive. We need not apologize when we proclaim love not lust and reject anything less than the best for men and women made in God's image.

2. In particular, pornography is anti-relationship and thus *anti-family*. Through its obsession with sexual function, pornography carefully avoids any recognition of the value of family relationships. Marriage is ridiculed, promiscuity promoted, homosexual relationships glamorized and group sex endorsed. Sexuality is integrally related to the family unit, and its use for non-relational gratification is wrong. One modest benefit arising from the flood of pornography is that, against the sharp alternative of the pornographic society, the value of biblical family ideals is even more clearly evident.

3. Pornography is *anti-human*. By its preoccupation with organs and functions, pornography departs from the representation of real people. Stories lack plots with character, pictures portray anatomy often without the face whereby a human being might be identified. By this subhuman approach, pornography dehumanizes. It treats sexual behavior between humans as of no greater significance than the copulation of animals. In fact, pornography presents sexual acts with animals as if they could be simply another variety of human experience. In Leviticus 18:23, such acts are condemned as "perversion."

4. Pornography is *anti-woman*. The outright degradation and humiliation of women are the central themes of pornographic stories and pictures. In soft pornography, the victimization is less obvious but nonetheless present, as women are treated as sex-objects, disposable creatures to be ogled, used and abused, and

then discarded in favor of another.

Many men who would resist the temptation to adultery and use of prostitutes will fall for the substitute of pornographic publications to provide sexual gratification. In view of Jesus' teachings about lustful thoughts (Mt. 5:28), it is difficult to see how this is any more defensible morally. So there is a need to alert people to the dangers of promiscuity expressed in fantasy as well as in behavior.

5. Pornography is *anti-children*. It creates an environment which is inimical to the psychological and moral development of children. It promotes a sexualization of *all* relationships, so that it has become almost impossible for adults to meet, hitchhikers to ride or women to be out alone without the situation being construed as an opportunity for physical sex. Children are developing their view of the adult world in this context. A great deal of sex education is seeking to indoctrinate them from their earliest years with an amoral acceptance of promiscuity. They are bombarded with adult sexual images long before they are emotionally prepared. Far worse, a sizeable number are more grossly exploited as models and prostitutes, as victims of incest and the attacks of child molesters. No one has produced credible evidence that any of these risks has been reduced since pornography openly began to promote such ideas. The Western world has not seen such deliberate and widespread abuse since the days of the Industrial Revolution, when children were physically maltreated in the mines and factories.

6. Paradoxically, pornography is *anti-sex*. To reject pornography is to take a stand *for* sex as a special way of expressing and deepening interpersonal commitment. Pornography fails to understand sex as a sacred gift intended for joy, intimacy and deep fulfillment in a loving, lasting relationship. Instead it makes a public spectacle of what should be intimate acts. It takes what should be deeply personal and exploits it commercially, thereby denying the dignity and spirituality of sex. It even undercuts any idea of sex being fun in relationships which are strong and secure.

Psychological analyses of the *Playboy* philosophy have emphasized that the preoccupation of such magazines with the physical aspects of sexuality arises not from satisfaction or pleasure but from attempts to counter deep-seated fears of true sexual encounter. Everything is kept superficial and undemanding; ideas of commitment or marriage are avoided or deliberately ridiculed. It is not surprising, therefore, that recent content analyses of *Playboy* magazine have shown an increasing use of violent themes.[2]

7. Pornography, by its influence on customs and conventions, is *anti-social*. Defenders of pornography will argue that the decision to read or see it is a private one, of no concern to anyone else. Yet all the indications are that use of pornography has social repercussions. Evidence is accumulating all the time concerning individuals whose anti-social behavior (including sex crimes and crimes of violence) has been triggered by pornography. Few will deny that there has been a real growth in the incidence of sex crimes in recent years. The result is tragic not only for the victims, but for society, as it becomes permeated by fear and suspicion. The availability of pornography is strongly implicated as one of the factors in the corruption of society.

Victor Bachy, professor of communications at the University of Louvain, Belgium, after examining what has happened in Denmark over the last decade, came to the conclusion that statistics are largely meaningless there. What really matters is the widespread and insidious corruption which spreads so much further than pornography itself. He describes Vesterbro, the porn center of Denmark:

> In Vesterbro, most of the shops are barely a facade. What counts is *the rest*. The sale of porno texts and pictures is allowed, but the realities are not, and their exhibition is forbidden.... All the necessary personnel is hired [from] among the socially handicapped and kept in place through the cement of drugs. The whole thing is managed, organised, kept under strict control by big bosses, high-class criminals, international gangsters and magnates of finance. The methods of recruiting the female personnel resemble those of international procurers and white-slavery.... The liberalisation of pornography has not created Vesterbro, criminals, drugs, procurement. It simply has, in this area of Copenhagen, permitted the installation of criminality at

the highest level. The disease that was prevailing has become a general cancer. The indirect consequences of the 1969 law might well be far more important and more serious than its direct effects.[3]

8. Pornography is *anti-environment*. It is paradoxical and illogical to become angry at pollution of the natural environment and remain unmoved at the tawdry, garish, obscene and embarrassing displays of pornography on newsstands, outside movie houses and in the daily newspaper advertisements. We recognize the hazards of mercury in our water, fertilizer in our food and smoke in the air we breathe. Ought we not equally to be concerned at the visual pollution which assaults anyone who walks through Times Square, Hollywood, Piccadilly Circus or to a lesser extent almost any city in the Western world?

Because the effects take such a long time to reveal themselves, it took a long time before people realized fully the dangers of auto exhausts and cigaret smoking. Scientific evidence has now conclusively demonstrated these dangers. So, too, long before the evidence demonstrates all the ill effects, we may respond sensitively to the creeping pornographic pollution which threatens to stifle conscience and corrupt behavior. And already the evidence is beginning to appear. Should we wait for the scientists' final proof (for it may never come), or shall we speak prophetically of the dangers of immorality?

In many places, the availability of pornography depends on the assumption that community standards have changed so that sensible mature citizens now accept its presence. There is really no evidence to sustain this position (polls of public opinion invariably indicate a wish for tighter controls[4]), but so long as responsible citizens remain silent, certainly the *appearance* of change is there. So long as the aggressive minority shout for removal of restrictions and the voice of decency remains muted, the politicians and legislators may be forgiven for believing there has been a change.

On the other hand, there probably *has* been a change in attitudes —even among Christians. That is one of the insidious consequences of environmental pollution. We all experience a tolerance shift, so that what was unacceptable five years ago becomes marginal today, while the marginal of yesterday is the normal of today. We should take note of this and examine to what extent standards have been subtly but significantly lowered.

9. Pornography is *anti-community*. A whole new multi-million dollar industry has developed to supply the insatiable and ever-changing demand for pornography. Because it panders to human weakness, exploiting authors, models, publishers, retailers and customers alike, it has largely fallen into the hands of syndicated crime. Through close association with drugs and prostitution, a whole criminal subculture has begun to flourish. Inevitably, bribery of law enforcement officers, corruption in high places and violence against those who speak out have become commonplace where pornography prevails.

Removing criminal sanctions against pornography has not helped, as many claimed it would. It has simply made it easier for the criminal subculture to monopolize the market, maintaining an outrageous profit margin at lower risk. The bright hopes that people would lose interest and behave responsibly if only they were not constrained by the law rests firmly on the humanist philosophy of the goodness of man, and denies the weaknesses of human nature. The biblical view of man as sinful could scarcely be more dramatically confirmed than by the escalation of corruption that has followed the removal of legal sanctions.

10. Pornography is *anti-culture*. Much debate has arisen over the assertion, made by its defenders, that pornography deserves the same protection as fine art and literature. One of the hallmarks of art is that it ennobles and enriches. Pornographic treatments typically degrade and destroy. Certainly there will be occasions when the effect, the possible cultural merit, of a particular work will be disputed. But the material classified as hard-core pornography makes no such pretensions.

One of the strongest objections to pornography is that it not only presents a distorted and false view of the world, but also, by its very presence, excludes more enriching presentations. Just as cancer cells multiply and overwhelm healthy cells, so art and literature are attacked by pornography. Theater owners claim it is difficult to screen family entertainment because of competition from salacious films. Novels may be rejected unless spiced with heavy sexual content. Radio City, New York, claims it has had to discontinue its family entertainment after twenty-five years due to pressures from pornographic centers in nearby Times Square. The Tivoli Gardens in Copenhagen, and the traditional fine theater and music of that city, lost patronage as sex shows and porno shops became a major tourist attraction. The promise that removal of legal restraints would lead to a flowering of culture has not been fulfilled. Indeed, as we have seen, men of culture rue the present impoverishment. There is little doubt that wide dissemination of pornography drives out true culture just as counterfeit currency drives out the true coin.

11. Pornography is *anti-conscience*. It is by conscience, enlightened by the Holy Spirit, that we become aware of the moral law of God and distinguish good from evil and right from wrong. Just as through constant exposure to violence in the media people lose sensitivity to real violence, so too our conscience can be blunted by pervasive pornography. We begin to accept the idea that people may be used as objects and that sex may be used indiscriminately. When we cease to care about the abuse of sexuality, we are losing concern for an essential part of human nature. If we are content with our own *personal* integrity and fail to care about the *social* impact of pornography, we may soon cease to care about other social problems as well—injustice and poverty, for example.

12. Pornography is *anti-God*. It is completely opposed to the teachings of Jesus about purity and love. His teachings set men and women free from enslavement to lust. Pornography, in the name of liberation, enslaves to an obsessive preoccupation with lust. Further, it deliberately attacks that which is sacred to the Christian faith. The violation of nuns, perversions practiced by priests and the use of churches for sacrilegious orgies are favored themes. The person of Jesus himself is desecrated by obscenity and blasphemy with the purpose of ridiculing Christian beliefs. The hate and anger directed against women in so much pornography is also vented against God himself.

When Danish pornographer, Jens Thorsen, proposed to make a pornographic film about Jesus Christ, the Christians of Denmark finally took action against what had been occurring for some years in that country. They said, "If we allow this, then as a country we deserve judgement." They fought and won. Others have done similarly. When an attempt was made to make the film in England, the producer was refused entry to the country. In an unprecedented way, through the initiative of concerned Christians, public reactions against the film came from the Prime Minister, the Archbishop of Canterbury, the Catholic Archbishop of Westminster and the Queen herself. Should we do less to protect the name of Jesus Christ?

Positive Christian Action
What shall we *do* then? Shall we band together as vigilantes and burn down sex shops? God forbid. Shall we develop an obsessive witch hunt against everything sexual and return to Victorian prudery? Impossible.

What we can do is develop a truly biblical view of sexuality and human relationships which will enable our own families to grow into maturity. But we need to go further if we care about the effect of pornography on the lives of others.

⚫ First, churches need to give sound teaching on sexuality within the church program, not just for engaged or married couples but for teen-agers too. Increasingly, sex education of a secular kind is hostile to Christian values and is fast becoming compulsory. We must not simply object to this denial of parental rights, but provide a balanced alternative. Sometimes, churches are able to make a stand against pornography in their locality. This is worthwhile but risky unless those who lead are theologically well informed and know how to express Christian views in a mixed society. The technicalities of legislation surrounding pornography are so complex and vary so much from place to place that it is wise to collaborate with those national bodies whose task is to coordinate and advise. Well-meaning but ill-judged protest may simply give free publicity to evil. Responsible action will avoid this.

⚫ Some Christians need to make it their special ministry to influence the media. Questions relating to the limits of art, literature, theater and television require experts to guide others to the appropriate response. Pornography itself is difficult for the average Christian to understand (especially the effect it can have on disturbed minds); so action should only follow careful study.

The most obvious response to pornography is to advocate censorship of such materials. In the light of the arguments put forward in earlier chapters, we should not be ashamed to advocate censorship. Nevertheless, this too is a complex legal and political issue. The very word generates a negative reaction.

But censorship alone cannot eliminate the problem of pornography. The ugly growth of pornography is nourished by human brokenness, spiritual and moral decay and a loss of values. Restraint of evil could certainly help, but we must also think preventively if in the long run we are to bring good. It was Alexander Solzhenitsyn who, in his already famous speech at the Harvard Commencement ceremony in 1978, said,

> Destructive and irresponsible freedom has been granted boundless space. Society appears to have little defence against the abyss of human decadence, such as, for example, misuse of liberty for moral violence against young people, motion pictures full of pornography, crime and horror. . . . Life organised legalistically has thus shown its inability to defend itself against the corrosion of evil.[5]

Rather than thinking along the traditional, restrictive lines implicit in the word censorship, we may do better to respond to pornography in terms of "quality control."[6] This concept is readily understood in industry. Commodities must reach a minimum standard or be rejected. A good factory sets and enforces its own standards; others, who seek to flood the market with inferior products, are increasingly subject to external controls, especially if there is potential danger to consumers. The emphasis throughout is not on the rejection of a substandard product but on preservation and protection of a quality product.

A similar approach might be taken to what we read and see. We must strive for excellence and argue for standards that take account of the psychological and moral impact of mass communications. We will be obedient to Christ's commission to be salt and light in the world as we seek responsibly to influence public opinion to reject the worthless in favor of the good.

Much of the debate on how society shall deal with pornography goes on in parliaments. The secular arguments receive full coverage. The politician who opposes pornography all too often receives little support. Another important role for Christians is supporting people in government who are arguing the case for restraints on pornography and for media responsibility in general. Sending information and letters of encouragement, and praying for these leaders are important ways of fighting pornography. There is little purpose in fulfilling Paul's instruction to *pray* for those in authority "that we may lead a quiet and peaceable life" (1 Tim. 2:2) unless we are prepared to *act* in such a way that these prayers can be answered.

We may summarize the Christian response with the aid of Professor E. M. Blaiklock's commentary on Romans 1:26-32, a passage in which Paul succinctly identifies the sexual temptations and practices of his day. Blaiklock writes:

The close of this chapter is a warning to all peoples and all ages. To read it in our own "permissive society" is to encounter a challenge to be strong in faith, determined in our committal to God, urgent in our evangelism. Paul is describing a society which had abandoned God. He is diagnosing the malady from which Rome was to die, for no great nation has ever been destroyed by a foe from without which has not already destroyed itself by corruption within. Such sin carries its own penalty, its own damnation. The time is here when Christians must show, as they were called upon to do in Rome, by word, act and manner of life, their difference.[7]

Notes

Preface
[1]John Stott in *Keswick Week 1972* (London: Marshall, Morgan and Scott), pp. 55-56.

Chapter 1: The Challenge of Pornography
[1]Lord Longford, *Pornography: The Longford Report* (London: Coronet Books, 1972), p. 412.
[2]Carl F. H. Henry, "Christian Personal and Social Ethics in Relation to Racism, Poverty, War and Other Problems," *Let the Earth Hear His Voice*, ed. J. D. Douglas (Minneapolis: World Wide Publications, 1975), pp. 1169-72.
[3]Ibid., p. 1182.

Chapter 2: The Case for Pornography
[1]V. B. Cline, *Where Do You Draw the Line?* (Provo, Utah: Brigham Young University Press, 1974) p. 188.
[2]C. B. Reifler, J. Howard, M. A. Lipton, M. B. Liptzin and D. E. Widmann, "Pornography: An Experimental Study of Effects," *American Journal of Psychiatry*, 128 (1971), 575-82.
[3]*Presidential Commission Report on Obscenity and Pornography* (New York: Bantam, 1970), Pt. 3, chap. 2, pp. 197-309.
[4]Cline, p. 191.
[5]B. Williams, *Report of the Committee on Obscenity and Film Censorship*, Cmnd. 7772 (London: H.M.S.O., 1979).
[6]W. C. Wilson, "Can Pornography Contribute to the Prevention of Sexual Problems?" (paper delivered to a 1976 symposium on sexual problems); and *The Prevention of Sexual Disorders*, eds. C. B. Qualls, J. P. Wincze and D. H. Barlow (New York: Plenum Press, 1978), p. 161.
[7]G. G. Abel, D. H. Barlow, E. B. Blanchard and D. Guild, "The Components of Rapists' Sexual Arousal" *Archives of General Psychiatry*, 34 (1977), 895-903.
[8]Quoted in *The Times*, London, January 30, 1976, p. 17.
[9]B. Kutchinsky, *The Effect of Pornography on Sex Crimes in Denmark* (Copenhagen: New Social Science Monographs, 1970), p. 101.
[10]R. Ben-Veniste, "Pornography and Sex-Crime: The Danish Experience," *Technical Reports of the Commission on Obscenity and Pornography*, (Washington: U.S. Government Printing Office, 1971), VII, 245-61.
[11]B. Kutchinsky, "Eroticism without Censorship," *International Journal of Criminology and Penology*, 1 (1973), 217-25.
[12]B. Kutchinsky, "The Effects of Not Prosecuting Pornography," *British Journal of Sexual Medicine* (April 1976), pp. 18-19. (Published under his name but in fact an editorial account of his work.)
[13]Ibid., p. 19.
[14]See, e.g., Friedrich W. Nietzsche, *Thus Spake Zarathustra*, trans. A. Tille (London: Dent, 1966) and *The Genealogy of Morals* (New York: Vintage Books, 1969).
[15]Hans R. Rookmaaker, *Modern Art and the Death of a Culture* (London: Inter-Varsity Press, 1970), pp. 131ff.
[16]Quoted in P. Saunders, *The Biblical Basis of Christian Morality*. An unpublished manuscript whose contents I acknowledge in developing this section.
[17]Francis A. Schaeffer, *Escape from Reason* (London: Inter-Varsity Press, 1968), pp. 64-65.

[18]W. R. D. Fairbairn, *Psychoanalytical Studies of the Personality* (London: Tavistock, 1952), quoted in D. Holbrook, *The Pseudo-Revolution* (London: Tom Stacey, 1972), pp. 88-89.

[19]R. Huntford, *The New Totalitarians* (London: Allen Lane, 1975), chap. 15.

[20]D. Boadella, *Wilhelm Reich: An Evaluation of His Work* (London: Vision Press, 1972), quoted in D. Holbrook, *The Pseudo-Revolution*, p. 151.

[21]P. Grosvenor, in *Pornography: The Longford Report*, pp. 177-78.

[22]M. Whitehouse, *Whatever Happened to Sex?* (London: Wayland Publishers, 1977), p. 12.

[23]J. Money, "Issues and Attitudes in Research and Treatment of Variant Forms of Human Sexual Behaviour," *Ethical Issues in Sex Therapy and Research*, eds. W. H. Masters, V. E. Johnson and R. C. Kolodny, (Boston: Little, Brown and Co., 1977), p. 126.

[24]L. Eickhoff, "Sex Education and Sex Practice," *Child and Family*, 13 (1976), 1.

[25]C. W. Haskell, *Pornography and the Christian* (Palmerston N., N. Z.: G. P. H. Print, 1976), pp. 12, 15-16.

Chapter 3: The Evidence Examined

[1]*Presidential Commission Report*, p. 58.

[2]The Hill-Link Minority Report, contained in the *Presidential Commission Report*, pp. 456-578, and published separately by Morality in Media, 487 Park Ave., New York City, New York.

[3]V. B. Cline, "The Scientists vs. Pornography: An Untold Story," *Intellect*, 104 (1976), 574-76.

[4]J. W. Drakeford and J. Hamm, *Pornography: The Sexual Mirage* (Nashville: Thomas Nelson, Inc., 1973).

[5]H. J. Eysenck and D. K. Nias, *Sex, Violence and the Media* (London: Maurice Temple Smith Ltd., 1978).

[6]J. H. Court, *Law, Light and Liberty* (Adelaide: Lutheran Publishing House, 1975).

[7]*Presidential Commission Report*, p. 58.

[8]K. Davis and G. N. Braucht, "Exposure to Pornography, Character and Deviance: A Retrospective Survey," *Technical Report of the Commission on Obscenity and Pornography*, (Washington D.C.: U.S. Govt. Printing Office, 1971), VII, 173-243.

[9]C. B. Reifler, J. Howard, M. A. Lipton, M. B. Liptzin and D. E. Widman, "Pornography: An Experimental Study of Effects."

[10]H. H. Schaefer and A. Colgan, "The Effect of Pornography on Penile Tumescence as a Function of Reinforcement and Novelty," *Behavior Therapy*, 8 (1977), 938-46.

[11]V. B. Cline, *Where Do You Draw the Line?* p. 229.

[12]B. Kutchinsky, "The Effect of Pornography: A Pilot Experiment on Perception, Behavior and Attitudes," *New Social Science Monographs* (1970), p. 97.

[13]R. Ben-Veniste, "Pornography and Sex-Crime: The Danish Experience"; and B. Kutchinsky, "Towards an Explanation of the Decrease in Registered Sex-Crimes in Copenhagen," *Technical Report of the Commission on Obscenity and Pornography*, VII, 245-61 and 263-310.

[14]V. Bachy, "Danish 'Permissiveness' Revisited," *Journal of Communication*, 26 (1975), 40-43.

[15]Williams, p. 83.

[16]*Presidential Commission Report*, p. 275.

[17]P. H. Gebhard, J. H. Gagnon, W. B. Pomeroy and C. V. Christenson, *Sex Offenders: An Analysis of Types* (London: Heinemann, 1965), p. 27.

[18]For example, R. Haney, M. H. Harris and L. Tipton, "Impact of Reading on Human Behavior," *Advances in Librarianship*, 6 (1976), 140-216.

[19]Eysenck and Nias, p. 114.

[20]T. P. Meyer, "The Effects of Sexually Arousing and Violent Films on Aggressive Behavior," *The Journal of Sex Research*, 8 (1972), 324-31.

[21]P. J. Tannenbaum and D. Zillmann, "Emotional Arousal in the Facilitation of Aggression through Communication," *Advances in Experimental Social Psychology*, ed. Leonard Berkowitz VIII (New York: Academic Press, 1975). Also, D. Zillmann, J. L. Hoyt and K. D. Day, "Strength and Duration of the Effect of Aggressive, Violent and Erotic Communications on Subsequent Aggressive Behavior," *Communication Research*, 1 (1974), 286-306.

[22]J. R. Cantor, D. Zillmann and E. F. Einsiedel, "Female Responses to Provocation after Exposure to Aggressive and Erotic Films," *Communication Research*, 5 (1978), 4, 395-411.

[23]R. A. Baron, "The Aggression Inhibiting Influence of Heightened Sexual Arousal," *Journal of Personality and Social Psychology*, 30 (1974), 318-22.

[24]R. A. Baron and P. A. Bell, "Sexual Arousal and Aggression by Males: Effects of Type of Erotic Stimuli and Prior Provocation," *Journal of Personality and Social Psychology*, 35 (1977), 79-87.

[25]Y. Jaffe, N. Malamuth, J. Feingold and S. Feshbach, "Sexual Arousal and Behavioral Aggression," *Journal of Personality and Social Psychology*, 30 (1974), 759-64.

[26]E. Donnerstein, M. Donnerstein and R. Evans, "Erotic Stimuli and Aggression: Facilitation or Inhibition," *Journal of Personality and Social Psychology*, 32 (1975), 237-44.

[27]Eysenck and Nias, p. 174.

[28]S. Feshbach and N. Malamuth, "Sex and Aggression: Proving the Link," *Psychology Today*, Nov. 1978, pp. 111-22.

[29]N. M. Malamuth, S. Feshbach and Y. Jaffe, "Sexual Arousal and Aggression: Recent Experiments and Theoretical Issues," *Journal of Social Issues*, 33 (1977), 110-33.

[30]Ibid., p. 121.

[31]Ibid., p. 126.

[32]Y. Jaffe, quoted in ibid., p. 116.

[33]Feshbach and Malamuth, "Sex and Aggression," p. 117.

[34]Ibid., p. 116.

[35]See "Children: Limits of Porn," *The Washington Post*, 30 Jan. 1977, p. C2.

[36]Eysenck and Nias, p. 174.

[37]R. S. Stoller, "Sexual Excitement," *Archives of General Psychiatry*, 33 (1976), 899-909.

[38]G. G. Abel, D. H. Barlow, E. B. Blanchard and D. Guild, "The Components of Rapists' Sexual Arousal," *Archives of General Psychiatry*, 34 (1977), 895-903.

[39]H. E. Barbaree, W. L. Marshall and R. D. Lanthier, "Deviant Sexual Arousal in Rapists," *Behaviour Research and Therapy*, 17 (1979), 215-22.

Chapter 4: The Benefits Analyzed

[1]W. C. Wilson, "Can Pornography Contribute to the Prevention of Sexual Problems?" *The Prevention of Sexual Disorder*, ed. C. B. Qualls, J. P. Wincze and

D. H. Barlow (New York: Plenum Press, 1978), pp. 159-79.
²Ibid., p. 176.
³J. Heiman, L. LoPiccolo and J. LoPiccolo, *Becoming Orgasmic: A Sexual Growth Program for Women* (Englewood Cliffs: Prentice-Hall, 1976).
⁴S. McMullen, "The Use of Film or Manual for Anorgasmic Women," *An International Conference*, ed. M. Cook and G. D. Wilson (Oxford: Pergamon, 1978); quoted in Eysenck and Nias, p. 196.
⁵P. Gillan quoted in Eysenck and Nias, pp. 196-99. See also her chapter, "Therapeutic Uses of Obscenity," *Censorship and Obscenity*, ed. R. Dhavan and C. Davies (London: Martin Robertson, 1978), pp. 127-47.
⁶Longford, p. 412.
⁷E. Kronhausen and P. Kronhausen, "The Psychology of Pornography," *The Encyclopaedia of Sexual Behavior*, ed. A. Ellis and A. Abarbanel (New York: Hawthorn Books, 1967), pp. 848-59.
⁸Feshbach and Malamuth, "Sex and Aggression," p. 117.
⁹For example, V. B. Cline, *Where Do You Draw the Line?*; J. H. Court, *Law, Light and Liberty.*
¹⁰J. H. Court, "Pornography—An Unfulfilled Dream." Research Report 35/76/6 to Criminology Research Council, Canberra, 1977.
¹¹*Presidential Commission Report*, p. 274.
¹²J. H. Court, "Pornography and Sex-Crimes: A Re-evaluation in the Light of Recent Trends around the World," *International Journal of Criminology and Penology*, 5 (1977), 129-57.
¹³V. Bachy, pp. 40-43.
¹⁴Rape report data received in a personal communication from the Police Department, Copenhagen, 1978.
¹⁵*The Viewer and Listener*, Winter 1979/80, p. 2.
¹⁶This relationship is discussed at length in my response to the Williams Report (in preparation).
¹⁷L. Radzinowicz and J. King, *The Growth of Crime* (London: Hamish Hamilton, 1977), p. 31ff.
¹⁸J. H. Court, "Rape and Pornography in Los Angeles." Paper presented to the Australian Psychological Society, Adelaide, 1977.
¹⁹D. Biles and J. Braithwaite, "Crime Victims and the Police," *Australian Psychologist*, 14 (1979), 345-55.
²⁰J. H. Court, "Pornography and Rape—Promise and Fulfillment." Research Report 35/76/7 to the Criminology Research Council, Canberra, 1977.
²¹M. Roth, "Sexual Pornography and Society: A Psychiatric View." Fifth Goodman Lecture delivered at the Royal Society, London, for the Society of Opticians, May 1977.
²²A. Bandura, *Principles of Behavior Modification* (New York: Holt, Rinehart and Winston, 1969), p. 193.
²³R. G. Geen, "Observing Violence in the Mass Media," *Perspectives on Aggression*, ed. R. G. Geen and E. C. O'Neal (London: Academic Press, 1976), pp. 193-234.
²⁴Ibid., pp. 220-21.
²⁵J. H. Court, *Law, Light and Liberty*, pp. 38-39.
²⁶D. Holbrook, *The Pseudo-Revolution*, p. 20.
²⁷Williams, Appendix 6, pp. 250-57.
²⁸*Washington Post*, 30 Jan. 1977, p. C2.

[29]*Christian Enquirer*, Oct. 1979, p. 11.

Chapter 5: The Philosophy Evaluated

[1]J. H. Court and O. R. Johnston, "Psychosexuality: A Three-dimensional Model," *Journal of Psychology and Theology*, 6 (1978), 90-97.

[2]*Sarnia Observer* (Canada), 30 Nov. 1976, p. 6.

[3]Siegfried Ernst, *Man, the Greatest of Miracles: An Answer to the Sexual Counter-evolution* (Collegeville: The Liturgical Press, 1976), p. 88.

[4]D. O. Moberg, *The Great Reversal* (London: Scripture Union, 1973), pp. 150ff.

[5]Aldous Huxley, *Brave New World* (London: Chatto and Windus, 1964), p. xv.

[6]P. A. Sorokin, *The American Sex Revolution* (Boston: Porter Sargent, 1957).

[7]R. Huntford, chap. 15.

[8]M. Whitehouse, *Whatever Happened to Sex?* p. 79.

[9]Phrase used by J. J. Ray in *Conservatism as Heresy* (Sydney: A. N. Z. Books, 1974), p. 143.

[10]Whitehouse, p. 107.

[11]For a discussion of Reich, see P. Boadella, "Pseudo-Sexuality and the Sexual Revolution," *The Case Against Pornography*, ed. D. Holbrook (London: Tom Stacey, 1972), pp. 144-56; and E. Chesser, "Orgasm According to Reich," *The Wonderful World of Penthouse Sex*, 3d. M. Vassi (New York: Warner Books, 1975), pp. 291-301.

[12]For a critique of Herbert Marcuse, see Erich Fromm, *The Crisis of Psychoanalysis* (Harmondsworth: Penguin, 1973), pp. 27ff.

[13]*Obeying Christ in a Changing World*, ed. B. Kaye, Vol. 3 of *The Changing World* (Glasgow: Collins, 1977); see especially chap. 4 "Marriage and the Family" by O. O'Donovan.

[14]Siegfried Ernst, *Man, the Greatest of Miracles*, p. 78.

[15]UNICEF, Declaration of the Rights of the Child, 1959.

[16]See, e.g., *Time*, 4 Apr. 1977, p. 53, and 28 Nov. 1977, p. 38; and "Children: A Big Profit Item for the Smut Producers," *Los Angeles Times*, 26 May 1977, Part II, pp. 1-5.

[17]C. W. Haskell, *Pornography and the Christian*, p. 12.

[18]Ibid., p. 13.

[19]Rollo May, *Love and Will* (London: Souvenir Press, 1970), pp. 57-61.

[20]*No, No, Calcutta*, ed. L. R. Shilton (Adelaide: Brolga Books, 1971), p. 33.

[21]M. Muggeridge, quoted in Longford, p. 412.

[22]D. Holbrook, *The Pseudo-Revolution* (London: Tom Stacey, 1972); *Sex and Dehumanisation* (London: Pitman, 1972); and *The Masks of Hate* (London: Pergamon, 1971).

[23]D. Holbrook, *Pornography and Hate* (London: The Responsible Society, 1972), p. 4.

[24]R. E. Kenyon, "Pornography, the Law and Mental Health" in *British Journal of Psychiatry*, 126 (1975), 225-33.

[25]R. Stoller, *Perversion: The Erotic Form of Hatred* (New York: Pantheon Books, 1975) p. 65.

[26]D. E. H. Russell, "Pornography: A Feminist Perspective," symposium paper (San Francisco, 1977).

[27]Susan Brownmiller, *Against Our Will: Men, Women and Rape* (New York: Simon and Schuster, 1975).

[28]W. King, "Punk Rock," *Newspage*, 1 (1977), (a newssheet published by Women against Violence in Pornography and Media, Berkeley, California).

[29]Open letter of concern from the Most Rev. Philip F. Pocock, Archbishop of Toronto, published in the *Globe and Mail*, 3 Dec. 1976.

[30]Bishop Cathal Daly, "Christianity and Sex," *New Zealand Tablet*, 100 (1973), p. 17.

Chapter 6: The Civil Liberties Case Evaluated

[1]In particular, the Keele Congress (1967) and Nottingham Congress (1977) of Evangelical Anglicans in England, and the Lausanne Congress (1974).

[2]Humanist Manifesto II in *The Humanist*, Sept.-Oct. 1973, and *Australian Humanist*, 28 (1973), 10-15. Both manifestos are published in book form as well: *Humanist Manifestos I and II* (Buffalo: Prometheus Books, 1973).

[3]Evaluations of this philosophy from a Christian perspective include G. Collins, *The Rebuilding of Psychology* (Wheaton, Ill.: Tyndale House, 1977), especially chap. 4; O. Guinness, *The Dust of Death* (London: Inter-Varsity Press, 1973), especially chap. 1; C. Harcourt-Norton, *Humanism: The Big Lie* (Sydney: Anglican Information Office, 1976); C. Martin, *How Human Can You Get?* (London: Inter-Varsity Press, 1973); J. W. Sire, *The Universe Next Door: A Guide to World Views* (Downers Grove: InterVarsity Press, 1977), especially chap. 4.

[4]A. Wertheimer, "Victimless Crimes," *Ethics*, 87 (1977), 302.

[5]Humanist Manifesto II, p. 12.

[6]A. P. Herbert, letter to *The Times* (London) 26 Aug. 1970, quoted in Williams, p. 16.

[7]I. Kristol, "Is This What We Wanted?" *The Case Against Pornography*, ed. D. Holbrook (London: Tom Stacey, 1972) pp. 187-94. See also a chapter in Cline's *Where Do You Draw the Line?* and a reprint in *Reader's Digest*, (Feb. 1975), pp. 129-32.

[8]Including John Stuart Mill himself and many of his contemporary followers, especially in relation to the portrayal of violence.

[9]M. Whitehouse, *Whatever Happened to Sex?* p. 13. See also the Williams Report, para. 9-38, p. 125.

[10]Speech by R. Brown. Proceedings in provincial parliament of British Columbia, June 21, 1977, pp. 2940-49.

[11]J. S. Mill, *On Liberty* (1859) in *Utilitarianism*, ed. M. Warnock (London: Fontana, 1962), pp. 126-40.

[12]Ibid., p. 135.

[13]H. Abelson, R. Cohen, E. Heaton and C. Suder, "Public Attitudes towards and Experience with Erotic Materials," *Technical Reports of the Commission on Obscenity and Pornography*, (Washington: U. S. Government Printing Office, 1970), VI, 1-121.

[14]See *The Los Angeles Times*, 26 May 1977, Section II.

[15]D. Maddison, "Mental Health in the Permissive Society," *Medical Journal of Australia*, 58 (1971), 908-14.

[16]Mill, p. 138.

[17]B. Cox, J. Shirley and M. Short, *The Fall of Scotland Yard* (Harmondsworth: Penguin, 1977).

[18]O. R. Johnston, "The Law of the Cinema," *Third Way*, 22 Sept. 1977, pp. 13-15.

[19]An exception is A. Comfort, *Sex in Society*, (Harmondsworth: Penguin, 1964), p. 76.

[20]M. B. Quanty, "Aggression Catharsis: Experimental Investigations and Implications," *Perspectives on Aggression*, ed. R. G. Geen and E. C. O'Neal (London: Academic Press, 1976), pp. 193-234.

[21]V. B. Cline, *Presidential Commission Minority Report* (1970), pp. 463-64.

[22]H. Abelson, et al., Op. cit.

[23]H. J. Eysenck, *Psychology Is about People* (Harmondsworth: Allen Lane, 1972), pp. 276-77.

[24]A Christian response to free circulation of pornography has been presented by Sir Frederick Catherwood in *The Longford Report*, pp. 138-49, and set in the broader context of Christian teaching on social issues in his *A Better Way* (London: Inter-Varsity Press, 1975). The relationship between morality and law in society is also the theme of J. N. D. Anderson's *Morality, Law and Grace* (London: Inter-Varsity Press, 1962).

[25]A. Wertheimer, p. 318.

[26]Humanist Manifesto II, p. 13.

[27]Basil Mitchell, *Law, Morality and Religion in a Secular Society* (London: Oxford University Press, 1970), p. 75.

[28]Martin Luther King, Jr., quoted in *The Longford Report*, p. 84.

Chapter 7: What Then Shall We Say and Do?

[1]For the headings in this chapter, I acknowledge the assistance of Rev. Fred Nile, National Director of the Australian Festival of Light.

[2]N. Malamuth and B. Spinner. A longitudinal content analysis of sexual violence in the best-selling erotica magazines. *Journal of Sex Research*, in press.

[3]V. Bachy, *Copenhagen, 1975*. Unpublished manuscript, 1978.

[4]See J. H. Court, *Law, Light and Liberty*, p. 52.

[5]A. Solzhenitsyn, "A World Split Apart." Commencement Address at Harvard University, 8 June 1978.

[6]J. H. Court, "Censorship—A Conservative Viewpoint," *Conservatism as Heresy*, ed. J. J. Ray (Sydney: A. N. Z. Books, 1974), pp. 314-35. See also "Pornography and the Public Good," *The Times* (London) 3 Aug. 1976.

[7]E. M. Blaiklock, *Daily Bible Commentary* (London: Scripture Union, 1973), pp. 27-28.